Metaphysics: The Light Side
A Beginner's Guide to Spirituality

CHARLES J. WEISS

Metaphysic: The Light Side
A Beginner's Guide to Spirituality

CHARLES J. WEISS

TONE CIRCLE PUBLISHING • NEW YORK

Published by Tone Circle Publishing, LLC
Copyright © 2011 by Charlie J. Weiss

Artwork by Anita Weiss

www.tonecircle.com

ISBN 978-0-9787264-2-3

Printed in the United States of America

Notice of Rights

All rights reserved. No part of this book may be reproduced or transmitted in any form by any means, electronic, mechanical, photocopying, recording, or otherwise, without the prior written permission of the publisher. For information on getting permission for reprints or excerpts, contact Tone Circle Publishing.

Table of Contents

ACKNOWLEDGMENTS   *v*
FOREWORD   *vii*
PREFACE   *xi*
INTRODUCTION   *xiii*

CHAPTER ONE -   1
LISTEN UP!

CHAPTER TWO -   4
WHADDA YOU KNOW?

CHAPTER THREE -   8
THE GRINNING MAN

CHAPTER FOUR   12
NOW YOU SEE IT -— OR DO YOU?

CHAPTER FIVE -   16
NOW YOU SEE IT...

CHAPTER SIX   21
LIVE TO EAT......EAT TO LIVE

CHAPTER SEVEN   27
HYLOZOISM

CHAPTER EIGHT   30
WHAT'S GOING ON HERE?

CHAPTER NINE   40
WHAT'S REALLY GOING ON HERE?

CHAPTER TEN   46
WHAT'S REALLY GOING ON HERE?

CHAPTER ELEVEN   51
TELL ME, CAN YOU FEEL IT?

CHAPTER TWELVE SO! WHAT DO YOU THINK?	58
CHAPTER THIRTEEN LET'S GET TO WORK	66
CHAPTER FOURTEEN THIS IS IT	72
CHAPTER FIFTEEN IF AT FIRST YOU DON'T SUCCEED	75
CHAPTER SIXTEEN WHAT GOES AROUND, COMES AROUND	79
CHAPTER SEVENTEEN ONE MORE TIME......	85
CHAPTER SEVENTEEN - IT'S LIKE THIS...	90
CHAPTER NINETEEN NOW WHAT?	94
CHAPTER TWENTY NOW YOU'VE GOT IT ... YOU THINK	98
CHAPTER TWENTY-ONE THINK ABOUT IT	101
CHAPTER TWENTY TWO THINK ON THESE THINGS	105
CHAPTER TWENTY-THREE YOU ASKED FOR IT	108
CHAPTER TWENTY-FOUR - WHAT DO YOU SAY?	116
CHAPTER TWENTY-FIVE - READ ANY GOOD BOOKS LATELY?	122
CONCLUSION	127

ACKNOWLEDGMENTS

Where to begin? I guess with Anthony J. Fisichella, Teacher, Lecturer and Author - my friend and mentor - the Tony that I mention in the book that told us to keep on keeping on "Until you get it right!"

I met Tony for the first time when I attended a lecture he gave at a library in Hicksville, New York many years ago. It was then that I was introduced to the "Ageless Wisdom." I was fascinated. Tony had an encyclopedic knowledge and understanding of the writings of Madame Blavatsky and Alice A. Bailey and any number of other sources in the field I call "Metaphysics" in this book. That night literally changed my life. It led me to devote myself to the study of these teachings, which when followed, becomes a better way of living and understanding life.

Tony had started a center in Hicksville called the New Age Center in which classes were given by Tony and other teachers with no charge. It was there, after much time and study, that I was able to begin my own teaching.

I moved to Blacksburg, Virginia, where I started teaching the classes mentioned in the Foreword of this book.

A number of the students from these classes were interested in further learning and we started a weekly study group which I conducted for a number of years.

I would like to thank a number of these students, who, by their participation, encouraged me to continue with my work, which eventually led to the writing of this book. Namely: Chuck Lynn; Dianne Rhody-Scott; Tom Shaw; Clarity James; Elizabeth White; Kathe Hansen; Sherri Songer; Patricia Carry-Smith; Dianne Rapp; Diane Owens; Nicolas Karamoun; Dan and Judi Schneck; Haricharandas; Steve Prupas; Jeb Rawnsley; Ed Weiss and all those that listened to my teachings down through the years.

And lastly, my beloved wife Anita, who contributed the art work to this book and who has been walking "The Path" by my side since the very beginning and supported me and encouraged me all along the way. I could not have written this book without her.

- Charles Weiss

FOREWORD

There is a Hebrew/Yiddish word that best describes what you are about to read ... the word is Seichel (pronounced, "sigh-'ch'ull," with a guttural 'ch'). As is the case with many such words, Seichel has no literal English translation that gives it justice. "Officially," the corresponding Hebrew word, Sheekool means, "discretion;" in Yiddish, Seichel means, "common sense." But neither one of these definitions really gets at the essence of the word ... which connotes a kind of wisdom that does not derive from having a degree from Harvard! One who is endowed with Seichel knows not only what is right, but also, what is smart ... and he or she did not gain such knowledge from books or guides [although, I admit, you are about to read, and hopefully, learn, from a book ... but a very different kind of book ... one that points you in the right direction, rather than teaches you cognitive skills]. Seichel connotes one's ability to get right to the heart of a matter ... cut through the irrelevant details, instinctively identify the essence of what needs to be done, automatically do exactly the right thing, solve problems in a timely manner to achieve practical, desirable, optimized results with the least amount of effort and the most amount of ordinary common sense. Seichel deals more with unfailing intuition than it does with any form of intellectual reasoning. But more than that, seichel is an intuition that employs practical knowledge and understanding of what works, as opposed to just "blind faith;" it falls into the same category as those attributes of an athlete that trainers claim "can't be taught or coached – it's just there!" Which brings me to the wisdom contained in this book.

In the Fall of 1997, my wife, Judi, and I registered to take a class in Metaphysics, taught by Charlie Weiss through the "Free School" of the YMCA at Virginia Tech. The title of the course caught our attention and piqued our interest. Mind you, you are "talking" to an individual who was graduated from four different Universities; who, in the process, amassed in excess of 300 college credits and four degrees, including a Ph.D. in Fluid, Thermal and Aerospace Sciences; an individual who spent 13 years as a student in various colleges and Universities; who, to this point in time, had been a student of the human body for almost 35 years, and for the past 25 of those years, was Head of the Biomedical Engineering Program at Virginia Tech. What could Charlie Weiss possibly teach me that I did not already know?

Well ... teach me he did! Without a doubt, "Metaphysics" turned out to be the most enlightening ... in the true sense of Seichel ... the most practical course I had ever had dealing with the whole of the human experience, to wit:

- I already knew that the drive for spiritual fulfillment was the third strongest of all human drives ... after the drive for survival of the self (first) and the drive for survival of the species (second, affectionately referred to as the "drive for sexual fulfillment"); but nobody had ever been able to define for me, exactly what this "drive for spiritual fulfillment" meant, really!

- I already knew that if I had learned anything about the human body, after 35 years of studying it (47+ years as I write this) ... I learned that we know very little about it! But nobody had ever been able to shed some light on that level of ignorance; to put it into perspective; to integrate into a whole, the omnifarious dimensions of the human experience at all levels of experienced "reality."

- I already knew that if we put a name on something, we fool ourselves into thinking we know what it is; but nobody had ever distinguished for me, in a meaningful way, the difference between labeling ["defining"] and understanding the essence of something ["describing"].

- I already knew that there is no such thing as an "unbiased" opinion about anything; but nobody had ever been able to put such skewing of attitude into perspective, to show me how to deal with it in a practical way.

- I already knew that all of those years in higher education had taught me how to make a living; but not a one of those 300+ credits had taught me how to live!

Charlie Weiss's class in Metaphysics embodies practical approaches to living effectively and meaningfully. He uses what I call, "Reader's Digest Language" to bring fundamental concepts down to earth in an uncomplicated way ... and he interjects humor in a very timely manner to "soften the landing." His insights are unique; he is approachable; his techniques of teaching are not intimidating; and some of his jokes are even funny! In short, Charlie Weiss's new text illustrates Seichel in action, and I am very happy to see it in print ... finally! Indeed, I am among the many who asked Charlie, "Is there a text book for this Course?" Now, there is!

Dr. Daniel J. Schneck
Professor Emeritus of Engineering Science and Mechanics
Emeritus Head of Biomedical Engineering
Virginia Tech

PREFACE

We live in a world today, of terrorist attacks; snipers; the fear of war; and, indeed, war bubbling just beneath the surface in many parts of the world. Our own nation has been drawn into war in Iraq and Afghanistan.

Now, more than ever, people are looking for reasons and explanations and understanding, for why the world is in the condition that it is in. Relying on pure faith to supply answers and the final solutions to our problems, are for some, not enough. They are seeking further, more tangible means to that end. Many have turned to a study of Metaphysics in the hopes that therein may lie the answers to the seeming chaos in the world.

Though they have come seeking in the right place, those in search of truth are still frustrated, because the books that exist on the subject are often too complicated and too difficult to follow, and so they give up. This little book has tried to be a straightforward, concise, easy to understand, and light-hearted introduction to this very important philosophy and way of life. We have worked our way, gradually and gently, from the Exoteric (outer world) to the Esoteric (inner world), and along the way touched upon a great number of interesting and helpful topics.

Metaphysics deals with the energies that underlie and drive the world that we live in and how these energies respond to what we think, say and do, which helps to create the circumstances of our lives. There is no thought, word, or deed that the Universe does not respond to and so it behooves us to learn more about these energies and learn to use them consciously. Unfortunately, most of us are unaware of these energies and how the use (or abuse) of them affects our lives, and so we use them unconsciously and haphazardly. Conscious and positive use of these energies will eventually lead to the salvation of this world and help us to lead happier, healthier, and more fruitful lives, filled with purpose and direction.

INTRODUCTION

I am interested in teaching how Metaphysics and Spirituality affects your life; indeed, how it actually is <u>a way of life</u>. I'm interested in explaining why we are here (the purpose of life); where we are headed (the goal of life); and what is the best way to get there (with the greatest understanding).

In addition to explaining the principles of Metaphysics, this book is also a "How To" book. It suggests simple instructions and techniques that will help you to use these underlying energies in your own life in a very positive and uplifting way.

This is an introductory book and though it uses a straightforward conversational approach, it still deals with the major concepts of Metaphysics and supplies a very solid foundation for further study in this very important philosophy, which will help us to make this world a happy, peaceful, loving place to live.

One of the finest teachers that I have ever studied with said, "In order to really teach something you have to first say what it is that you're going to teach, then teach it, and then explain what you just said."

You might ask what the point is of listing the topics that you are going to cover because that would be in the table of contents. As you will see, the chapter headings don't give you a clue most of the time.

Before I go ahead and list the topics, I think it might be a good idea to attempt to define Metaphysics. Notice I said attempt! As far as I know, the prefix "meta" means "beyond" or "transcending." In that context, the word Metaphysics would mean "beyond physics" — which is still somewhat meaningless. This may be true, but it doesn't help us very much. Metaphysics is sometimes described as "The Science of Esotericism." Since the word esoteric means hidden, this hardly clarifies things, so I looked up Metaphysics in the American Heritage Dictionary, and, to my surprise, found something resembling what Metaphysics is actually about. Of course, if you don't already know what Metaphysics is about, this definition is definitely lacking. Here it is: "The branch of philosophy that examines the nature of reality, including the relationship between mind and matter, substance and attribute, fact and value."

What do I say? I say I'm not going to attempt to define Metaphysics, but instead, I'll tell you something about it. Metaphysics posits that there are energies at a vibrational level that go beyond what is measurable in the physical world, either through personal observation or through mechanical means, that is, instruments capable of sensing and reading very subtle energies. Furthermore, this world about us is an outward manifestation of these energies. So, it follows that the more we can understand about these energies the greater will be our understanding of the world around us. I'm not going to present highly technical information with complex mathematical formulas. I'm going to present the very practical aspects of these energies and give you some tools to work with them so you can put them to use in your own life. Since they are difficult to measure, the only way you are going to know if what I tell you is true or not is for you to work with these tools and see what happens. Experiment. Prove it or disprove it, but you have to be persistent and consistent. Don't come to me and say," I tried it once and it didn't work." If Edison had used that approach, you would be reading this in the dark.

So, what are the topics I'm going to cover in this book? In no particular order, here they are:

* What you think you know and what you actually do know
* The Higher Self and the lower self
* The "Real" and the "Unreal"

Introduction

* Esoteric and Exoteric
* Kirlian photography
* The Human Aura
* Prana and health - The Vital, or Etheric body
* Diet and Prana
* Hylozoism - the theory that everything is alive
* The Findhorn Gardens - growing huge vegetables in barren soil
* Cleve Backster - telepathic communication with plants
* Edgar Cayce
* The Seven Planes of existence
* How God created the world
* The Astral, or emotional Plane and how to purify the Astral Body
* The Mental Body, Thought-forms and how they affect your life
* Being "The Observer" and taking control of your life
* The "As-if" and the "Affirmation" technique to help purify your lower self
* The purpose of life - why we are here and where we are going
* The "real" Evolution - an evolution of consciousness
* To be Perfect -"as your Father in Heaven is Perfect" (Matthew: 5:49)
* Karma and Reincarnation
* Some questions answered about Reincarnation
* The story of Theodora and the removal of references to Reincarnation in the Bible
* The "Masters", or "Ascended Beings" and the "Kingdom of Heaven"
* Meditation - a tool for spiritual growth
* "Walking the Path" (to Perfection). Three things to help you along the way: Study - Meditate - be of Service
* Prayer and Affirmation

If you don't know what some of thus stuff is, or any of it, for that matter, that is why you are reading this book.

As you can see, there are many topics that Metaphysics deals with that come under the heading of "Psychic Phenomena." I want you to realize that these are side issues, and while they may be interesting, they are not the main thrust of this philosophy. I have seen too many people get caught up in the phenomena and become side- tracked. The time that you have to spend in this life is too valuable to waste it in that manner.

One last thing. This work begins with one premise: That there is a Great Creative Being who has been called by many names: God; The Most High; The Almighty; Lord, etc., and described in many ways: Infinite, Omniscient, Omnipresent. He has created this Universe for a Grand Purpose. We may see some glimmerings of that purpose, and seek to align ourselves with that purpose, since the Universe appears to be governed by unalterable Law, and not by whimsy.

I am not going to "prove" the existence of God, but I think that this study will demonstrate that existence — that we live in a universe of Cosmos and not Chaos.

I will sometimes quote from some of the great religious leaders and teachers, however, this book and this philosophy are non-sectarian. But, in as much as these men were teachers of the Law, when I quote Buddha or Jesus, it is to illustrate a point of the Law as taught by these great men.

The first several chapters will attempt to lay the groundwork for our discussion of Metaphysics. I think you will find these chapters to be both valuable and interesting. So much so, that if you get nothing else out of this book, our preliminary discussion might give you a slightly new (and better) approach to looking at the world around you.

METAPHYSICS: The Light Side

Figure 1 - The Wandering Mind

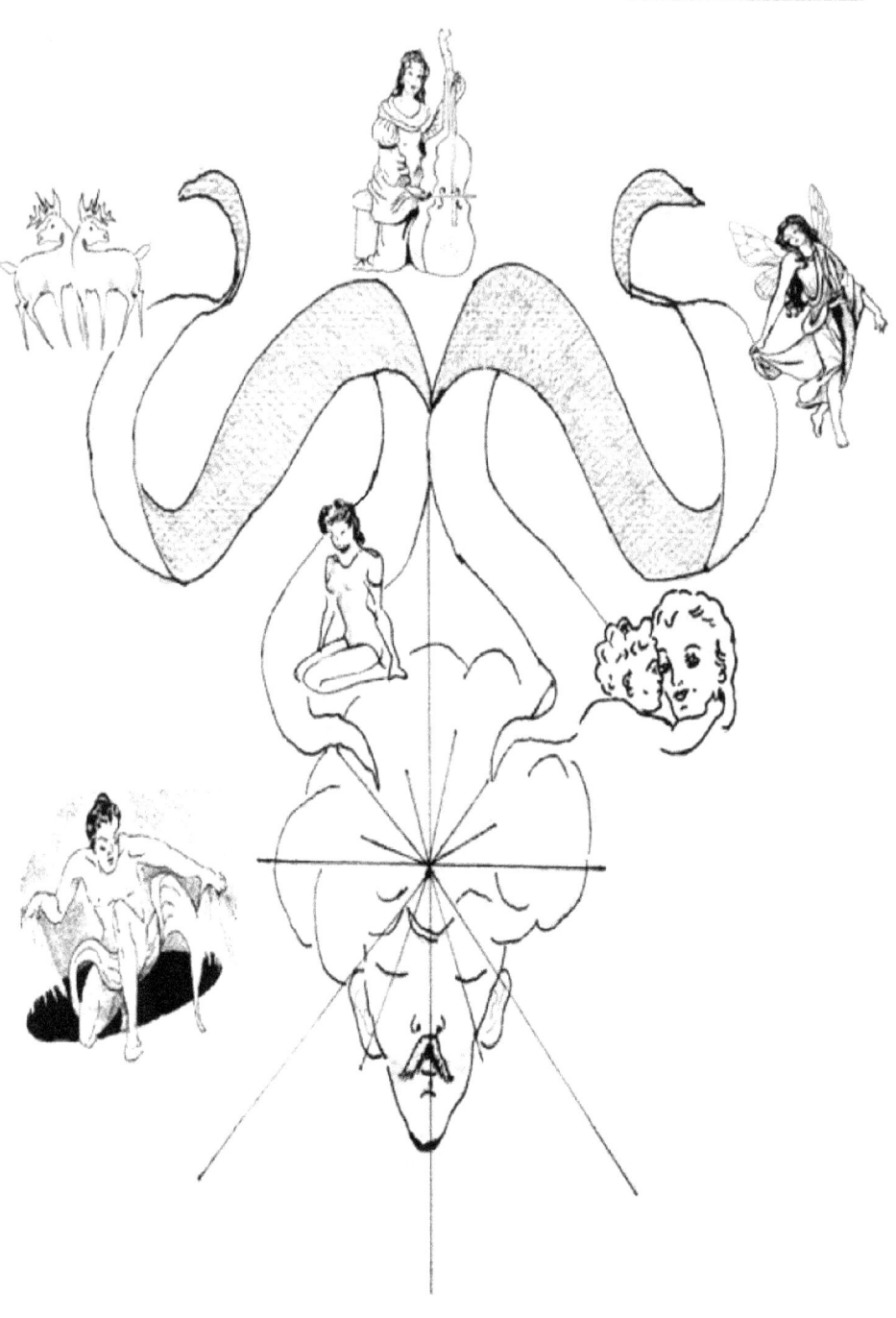

CHAPTER ONE - LISTEN UP!

It seems that one day a man was walking down a road and observed another man beating a donkey over the head with a stick. The first man approached the other and asked him what he was doing, whereupon the second man said, "I'm trying to teach him something." The first man, who was by now a bit agitated said, 'You can't teach anybody anything by beating them over the head with a stick. The second man replied. "I know that, but before I can teach him anything, I first have to get his attention."

Have I got your attention?

A number of years ago, the well-known Indian philosopher, Krishnamurti was giving a lecture at Carnegie Hall in New York. There were well over a thousand people that had come to hear the great man speak, and when Krishnamurti took the stage the audience waited in hushed anticipation. Krishnamurti stood quietly for a moment, just looking out at his audience, and then he spoke. He said, "I'm not going to tell you people anything, because you don't know how to listen."

There was a murmur in the audience and people glanced at one another quizzically. Some of them had traveled a great distance and had gone to considerable trouble to be there. They did not know what to make of what Krishnamurti had just said. Some people were annoyed, thinking to themselves, "I know how to listen." Some were just puzzled.

Krishnamurti continued, "No, you don't know how to listen. When someone speaks to you or you are reading a book, what you do is listen to your own thoughts. You take my words and you lay them against your own thoughts. If what I say happens to agree with those thoughts, then you think, "This Krishnamurti is alright, he is a wise man." If what I say disagrees with those thoughts, then you think, "Why did I bother coming here? This man does not know what he is talking about."

Krishnamurti went on to say that what he expected of the audience was that they would listen to what he had to say without judging what was being said one way or another, but to simply listen, so that what was being presented would not be interfered with.

So, I now repeat what Krishnamurti said. Many of the concepts presented in this book may be new to you, and some may even disagree with some of your cherished beliefs. Just listen. Initially accept everything you read, remembering that acceptance does not necessarily mean agreement, but it does imply "not rejecting." There is a tendency to react negatively when new information disagrees with "what you think you know." You reject it. Albert Einstein said, "Condemnation without investigation is the height of ignorance." One can be very bright and still be ignorant of the facts.

What if I were to offer you a book and say to you that it contained all of the wisdom of the ages. Would you accept such a book? Would you reject it? If you rejected it without investigation then you would have no chance of ever seeing its contents and you would remain ignorant. If you accepted it, that does not mean that you would automatically know everything that it contained, but at least you would be able to look at it, examine it — and perhaps — learn from it. That's what I mean by acceptance.

Don't you see that if you keep listening exclusively to your own thoughts, then you are on a path that leads you right back to where you started! You can't possibly learn anything beyond what you already think you know.

Another trick that your mind plays is to start wandering off onto all kinds of side paths. This mental wandering can be triggered by just a single word, and then, off you go (see Figure 1). If you are attending a lecture, you miss whatever is being said while your mind is on this little journey. At least with a book you can go back and reread what you missed.

So, Listen Up! We're off and running.

CHAPTER TWO
WHADDA YOU KNOW?

This is a true story. It sounds like a joke. I'm sure it is a joke, though it was not meant to be, but it actually happened. Many years ago I was working in, of all places, an aircraft factory. It was in the winter and I innocently said to no one in particular, "It feels like snow." If you've never heard that expression, what I meant was, "It feels like it's going to snow." Whereupon this fellow pipes up, "Nope, it's not going to snow. It's too cold to snow." So I said. What do you mean, it's too cold to snow? "Just what I said," he replies, "It's too cold to snow." "Does it snow in Alaska?" I asked? "Does it snow at the North Pole? At the South Pole? In the Himalayan Mountains?" I was sure that I had him. "Yup", he agreed, "It snows in all those places, but it's not gonna snow here and now because it's too cold to snow." "But isn't it a lot colder in those places that I just mentioned, and doesn't it snow there?" I shouted because by this time I was becoming aggravated. (Don't hold this against me, I didn't know any better way back then). And, of course, his reply was, "IT'S TOO COLD TO SNOW!" The story doesn't quite end there. About an hour later, it began to snow quite heavily. Triumphantly, I searched for and found this guy, pointed at the snow and said, "Aha!" with this big grin of victory on my face, "See the snow? It's snowing. It's snowing." Whereupon he said to me knowingly, "Yup, temperature must have gone up."

Chapter 2

A couple of times I've alluded to "What you think you know." This would seem to imply that I think that you don't really know what you think you know. Well, let me set the record straight. I am not implying that — I am saying it outright. You don't really know what you think you know.

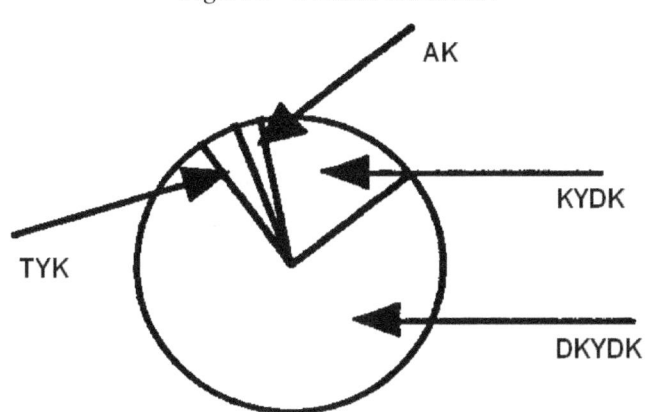

Figure 2 - Whadda You Know?

Lets examine Figure 2. Imagine that this is a pie that represents all that there is to know in the Universe. The two small pieces of the pie to the left are what you think you know (TYK). The smaller of those two pieces is what you actually know. (AK). The slightly larger piece to the right is what you know that you don't know (KYDK). For example, I know that I don't know how to build a diesel engine, or design a computer, etc. etc. Then what is the large piece of this pie? This is what you don't know that you don't know! (DKYDK).

What I'm saying is that there is a whole bunch of stuff out there that you don't even know exists. That's the piece of the pie that we're going to try to cut into and add it on to the piece that you actually know.

In order to see what I'm getting at here, you have to be absolutely honest with yourself and examine your belief system closely. Where did it come from? How much is something that you were just told by your parents, uncles, aunts, teachers, clergyman, peers, when you were too young to reason it out for yourself and you just grew up believing that it was so. For example, "It's too cold to snow." In other words, what have you been conditioned to believe and what have you actually experienced for yourself?

Consider this: First, if you believe something to be so, it's just a belief and it may or may not be so. If I believe that there are little green men living on the other side of Mars, it's just a belief and may or may not be so. Second; the only way you really know something is to experience it yourself. You can be told a hundred times that if you put your hand in the fire, it's going to get burned, but you won't know that is so unless you put your hand in the fire yourself. You may make certain assumptions based on past experience. For example, I don't have to slam my fist into a brick wall to know that it's going to hurt if I do that, because I've had the personal experience of falling down and scraping my knee on something hard, and I know that hard things can hurt. Let's go back to the fire again. You know through past experience with hot things, that if you put your hand in the fire, it will get burned. Right? If anybody puts their hand into a fire, it will get burned. Right again? Then how come there are Yogis who can put their hand in a fire, leave it there for awhile, and upon withdrawing it, their hand may look a little pink, but that quickly fades away and they are not burned.

We're not going to go through the whole process that the Yogi must go through to achieve that, but I do want to point out that because his experience is different than ours, he knows something very different than what you and I know, namely, that if he puts his hand in a fire it will not get burned.

There must be some serious self-examination here. You have to think about the things that you think that you know and see if you really know them. The Russian philosopher, Gurdjieff, said that people are always offering opinions about things that they know nothing about.

Here's a little homework assignment for you. Listen to other people's conversations and discussions and see if you think Gurdjieff is right or not. More difficult: see how many times you are about to offer an opinion about something that you know nothing — or at least, very little about.

What I'm talking about here is what I call your "Body of Truths." The things that you think you know and accept as truths, and how you conduct your life accordingly. At best, some of these things are actually true, but that's at best. Most likely a great number of these things are just beliefs — or worse — perhaps they are actually falsehoods that you've been conditioned to think are truths. This is where the self-examination comes in. You must be honest with yourself. This exercise may teach you some things about yourself that you never knew before.

One important point here: never get down on yourself. View your thoughts objectively as if you were an Observer. We'll talk more about being the Observer later on.

CHAPTER THREE -
THE GRINNING MAN

This is the parable of the grinning man. You know what a parable is. It's one of those stories that is told to confuse you because it's really about something else, and it was designed so that everyone can have their own interpretation and they can argue about it for 2000 years. Well, this is not one of those parables. It may be about something else, but it is not meant to confuse you, it is meant to enlighten you — but, that's what they all say, isn't it?

There once was a man who came to a certain door of a certain house and the man knocked on the door of the house and waited for a reply. There was no response, so the man knocked again, a little bit louder this time. All at once he heard a voice from the other side of the closed door. "Go away," the voice said, "there's nobody here." The man started to turn away, when he realized to himself, "Wait a minute. There must be someone there, otherwise there would be no one to say, "Go away, there's nobody here."

So the man turned back to the certain door of the certain house and he knocked again, even louder than the time before. Again he heard the voice: "Go away. Didn't I already tell you that there is nobody here?"

The man was certain by this time that there really was somebody there, so he knocked again....LOUDER! "I know you're in there," he said, "I can hear you saying: "There's nobody here," and that means there must be somebody there, and I have something very important to tell you."

Chapter 3

"Go away! Go Away! Go away!" said the voice from the other side of the door. "There's nobody home. There's nobody here and there won't ever be anybody here."

Whereupon the man turned sadly away from the certain door of the certain house and went to a different door of a different house. "Perhaps I'll have better success at this house," he thought to himself.

This time he didn't even have to knock. The door was wide open and a man with a big grin on his face invited him in. "Come in, come in," he said, "my door is always open." So the man began to tell the grinning man all kinds of things about the secrets of the universe and to everything the man had to say, the grinning man responded with a big grin and a nod of his head. "This is wonderful," the man thought to himself, "this grinning man accepts everything I have to say about the secrets of the universe. He knows. He understands." But then an odd thing happened. The man said something that was absolutely wrong and much to his surprise and chagrin, the grinning man continued nodding his head and grinning his great big grin.

Now the man began to deliberately speak all kinds of falsehoods and absurdities and the more he spoke, the more vigorously the grinning man grinned and nodded his head until finally the man, exasperated, turned sadly away once again as he realized that he had no more success with the grinning man than he did with the voice that said, "Go away, there's nobody here."

The man, although discouraged, continued going to certain doors of certain houses, having the faith that one day he would find a house where the voice would inquire as to who was there, and he would be invited in to speak to someone who did not have quite such a big grin; who would listen carefully, and occasionally, even ask a question or two about what was being said.

One good thing about this parable, is that since I wrote it, I know the message that I intended to communicate, and it will be so clear that even 2000 years from now, people will know its meaning.

— Interpretation —

The man who was going around from certain doors in certain houses, to different doors in different houses, represents the Higher Self of each individual: that part of ourselves which is the true "Knower," and is always attempting to reach us and teach us the truth.

Our Higher Self keeps knocking on the door of our lower consciousness, but, as in the case of the first man who kept saying, "Go away, there's nobody here," the Lower Self is so shut off from the Higher Self that the Higher Self cannot get through to it at all. The Higher Self may just as well have saved His time and His knuckles, because there was nobody home, even though the Lower Self is always home. This man had a completely closed mind. He would not accept the gift that the Higher Self was offering.

In the case of the second man, he was so open-minded that he was ready to listen to anybody and everybody, but he was unable to tell what information was coming from his Higher Self and what was coming from the Lower Self. In other words, he was not able to judge between what is true and what is false. He was ready to accept everything, and, as we have already said, accepting is not rejecting. Having an open mind is great — as long as your brains don't fall out. We must be able to discriminate between what is valuable and what is not, but the grinning man could not. (I hear that he has recently purchased some swamp land in Arizona and a piece of the Brooklyn Bridge). The Higher Self will never cease in His efforts to make contact with the lower self, and so, He keeps on trying until contact is finally made and the lower man may then proceed along his path of evolution.

Let's do a brief summary of the main points that we have covered so far:

1. In order to listen properly, it is necessary to put aside our thoughts, and the things that we "think we know," temporarily.
2. We need to realize that the only things we can truly know are what we experience for ourselves.
3. We must adopt an attitude of "acceptance" with the understanding that acceptance does not necessarily imply agreement.
4. We must then, at a later time, examine what we have heard, trying to get a sense of what we think may be valuable. And, to discriminate, to the best of our ability, between what feels like the truth and what does not; holding back on any final decision until we have the experience that lets us know for certain which is which.

CHAPTER FOUR
NOW YOU SEE IT — OR DO YOU?

I don't know if I am a man dreaming that I am a butterfly, or a butterfly dreaming that I am a man - Lao Tzu

The Eastern philosophies speak of the Real and the Unreal or Reality versus Illusion. Generally, they characterize the world as Unreal, or as an Illusion. We have difficulty with that concept because the world around us seems all too real. It's solid. It has existence. How can they say that it is illusion? Is it all in the eye of the beholder? Perhaps we can ask Max:

There was a very famous tailor living in New York who was said to make the finest suits in the city. In order to get a suit made by Abe, the Tailor, you had to put your name on a very long waiting list. Max was on such a list. He knew that Abe, the Tailor, was very expensive, but he thought it would be worth it just to be able to show the suit off to his friends and say, "This suit was made by Abe, the Tailor." And, of course he would actually have a suit made by the most famous tailor in all the land. If he was the best in New York, it followed he must be the best in all the land. Anyway, that's what New Yorker's say.

Finally, Max's turn had come. He had gone to Abe the Tailor, and Abe had measured him up. He called just this morning to say that the suit was ready and Max should come by and pick it up.

Max was very excited when he entered Abe the Tailor's shop. Abe held up the finished suit for Max to admire and you could see that it was made of the finest materials. Max

Chapter 4

went into the fitting room and tried on the suit. He came out of the fitting room and he could tell that some things were not quite right. "Abe," he said, the sleeve, it's a little too long on the right side." Abe said, "It's not the sleeve. You have to lift up your shoulder and stretch out your arm and it will fit perfectly." "But the back," Max said, "it's pushed out in the back." "No problem," says Abe, "just hunch up your back and lean forward a little bit." "But the jacket doesn't close right in the front," says Max, whereupon Abe replies, "Just twist your left side forward and down a little bit and it will be perfect." Max follows these instructions and Abe is now satisfied that it is a perfect fit.

Max was now walking down the street wearing his new suit. His right shoulder was lifted up with his right arm stretched out, his back was hunched up, and he leaned slightly forward with his left side twisted forward and down a little bit. As he made his way down the street he bumped into an old acquaintance named Marvin. "How do like the suit?" asked Max, "It was made by Abe the Tailor. Isn't he a wonderful Tailor?

Marvin walks all around Max and examines the suit very carefully. Finally, nodding his head as he speaks, Marvin agrees, "Yes, he'd have to be to fit a cripple like you."

What's real and what's illusion? Things are not always what they appear to be. To Max, the suit was perfect. To Marvin, Max was a cripple; and to Abe...well, who knows what Abe was thinking? The Eastern philosopher will say, "Who cares what they thought? None of it is Real. It's all an Illusion."

Let us take a little mental journey back in time. A time before Television, before Radio, before the Wireless, even before the discovery of electricity and magnetic fields. Way back in time to primitive man. What is Real to this primitive man? What he can see is real What he can touch is real. (Alright, this goes for the primitive she's also.) What she can see. What she can touch. (Okay if I go back to the he's?) What he can smell is real. What he can taste. What he can hear. Basically, whatever he can experience through his five senses is what he Knows is Real. We call this the *exoteric* world: the world around us.

Sure, he knows that there are things he doesn't know: like why the wind blows, why it rains, why there is thunder and lightning, and any number of other things. But, if someone were to tell him that people would one day communicate with each other over long distances, or that you could turn on a little box and listen to music, he would think you were crazy. All of the things that we take for granted today would be *esoteric* to primitive man, part of the things that *he didn't know that he didn't know*.

We have two worlds then: an *exoteric* world, which can be experienced by the five senses or extensions to those senses, such as, microscopes, telescopes, etc.. There are many for whom the objective exoteric world is the only world. The other world is *esoteric*: that which cannot be easily experienced by the senses. It is a hidden world that may require a sixth sense, or perhaps a seventh or eighth sense. There may one day be instruments that will enable us to experience the esoteric world directly. No doubt, we will seem like cavemen to men of the future. Even today, there is so much that we don't know that we don't know.

Consider this for a minute. Nothing in this world has any meaning other than that which we ascribe to it. We give each thing a label, which is just a name that identifies it. We call it tree, chair, couch, potato, television, etc. But what are all these things really? What is the Reality? What is the truth? Science explains the Reality of things as congregations of atoms, with a nucleus and electrons flying about. If you take any object and examine it under a super microscope, you will find that it is made up of huge numbers of atoms, kind of "hanging out" together. But, according to the Eastern philosophies, the world's things are just Illusion. We may think of them as solid and substantial "things," each with its own name, but, in fact, each thing is reducible to different collections of atoms that do not really have any meaning other than what we ascribe to it. As I have said earlier, things may not be what they appear to be.

What happens is that to most people, the world around them is the only Reality. But there are actually grades of Reality. Things of the mineral world seem the most Real. Our senses tell us that rocks are solid. You can feel it. You can get knocked out by it if it hits you over the head. Then there's the world of liquid things, which are not quite as substantial as solid things. Liquid can't even hold its own shape. Next, the gaseous world, which, if not for the mysterious force of gravity, its components would go flying out into space. Gases are even less substantial than liquids. Science informs us that all atoms, no matter what name we give the different collections of atoms, are made up of even smaller particles called protons, neutrons, electrons, etc. All these particles are comprised of even smaller components called quarks and leptons. So, the objects that appear real to us: a tree, a glove, a man, etc., are really descriptions of just one layer of reality.

The exoteric material world reflects into the esoteric spiritual world. Einstein equated Matter and Energy with his famous formula, $E = mc^2$. If m stands for *mass* (which is the weight of matter), and c^2 describes the fastest thing known to mankind (the speed of light squared), then we can think of Energy as Matter that is moving really, really fast. We might call the lower vibrations, Matter, and the higher vibrations, Energy. Another way of saying it is; Matter is Energy at its lowest vibration, and Energy is Matter at its highest vibration.

One more thing for you to think about before we move on: if we do indeed live within the different layers of an Infinite Being, how can we say that we will be able to measure the upper limits of vibration, given the finite limitations of our physical world instruments. If we live in an Infinite Being, shouldn't those vibrations go on into the Infinite? You can't measure the Infinite with the finite! More on this subject later.

CHAPTER FIVE -
NOW YOU SEE IT...

*We don't know a millionth of one percent about anything
- Thomas Edison.*

In the last chapter I demonstrated to you that as time goes on and technology increases, that more and more of the Universe around us is revealed. That which was esoteric becomes exoteric.

Don't let science fool you into thinking that all has been discovered. It hasn't. Science does not know what gravity is. Science does not really understand what electricity or magnetism are. Science knows how to use these things, and it can tell you about the rules that govern them. It can even give you mathematical formulas to describe them, but science is just getting its first clues about how all the energy and matter in the universe is organized into the unified tapestry that we call God.

In the past 50 years, there has been great progress in understanding various components and layers of Reality. With respect to the four forces of nature describing the interactions of matter, science has discovered that *gravitons* hold planets together with gravity; *gluons* hold nuclei together with the *strong* force, while the *electroweak* force breaks nuclei apart through radioactive decay; and finally, the *electromagnetic* force enables human beings to function by giving them light to see, sounds to hear, electricity for power, etc..

As I introduce the study of Metaphysics, my approach will be to move gradually and logically from the exoteric, objective world to the esoteric, subjective world. It will be a step by step, logical approach that attempts to understand and work with the Laws of this hidden world. It must be logical because God has to make sense. I expect people to make sense and I certainly should not expect anything less of the Great Being that we call God. One of the world's most famous and respected clairvoyants, a man named Charles Leadbeater, who lived in the early part of the 20th century, said when discussing God and the Laws of Metaphysics: "Let us be reasonable." That is what I hope to do.

The subject of this chapter is Kirlian Photography. About forty-five years ago, a Russian by the name of Semyon Davidovitch Kirlian published an article in the Russian Journal of Scientific and Applied Photography about a camera that he had developed to photograph the corona discharge of a human being, or what is more commonly called the Human Aura. In 1974, the Soviet government awarded Kirlian the title of Honored Inventor. Further information about Kirlian Photography and examples of Kirlian photographs may be found in the book "Rainbows of Life" by Mikol Davis and Earle Lane published by Harper and Row.

What makes Kirlian Photography of special interest to us is that these photographs demonstrate the existence of the Human Aura which up to this point was seen only by psychics and clairvoyants. Any mention of this was always met with a large dose of skepticism, especially by the scientific community.

The Human Aura is considered to be a field of energy that surrounds each and every human being. This description is not quite accurate, but I'll get to that in a minute. Metaphysicians have claimed the existence of this energy field for thousands of years and Kirlian came along and changed what had been esoteric for so long and brought it into the realm of the exoteric. There are those who still doubt the existence of this energy field even with the proof staring them right in the eyes. What's the expression? "There are none so blind as those who will not see."

Or, perhaps we can explain their skepticism this way: Where there's a will, there's a way. If there's a way, then there must be another way. If your wont is to take the other way, then I guess it follows that where there's a will, there's a won't. That was a little pun that I couldn't resist. Some people say that all puns are bad. I would agree, except for the ones that are good ones.

I said that the description of the Aura being an energy field that surrounds the body was not quite accurate. In Metaphysics, our understanding is that the Human Aura is actually made of several subtler bodies which are visible to the clairvoyant. These bodies vibrate at a much higher frequency than our physical body, and the atoms of these other bodies interpenetrate the atoms of the physical. And, because they are less dense, they expand out further than the physical body and thus seem to be energy fields surrounding the physical body. There are three such subtle bodies, two of which we will discuss later.

The one that I would like to discuss now is the one that is photographed by the Kirlian camera. This body is called the vital body or the etheric body. Etheric here is not to be confused with what the scientists call the ethers. The vital, or etheric body, is the one that is most closely tied in with the physical body. It is, of course, part of the physical world, but it is not yet measurable by our instruments, and can only be seen in Kirlian Photographs.

Before I continue, there are a couple of things that you should know about Kirlian Photography. The camera is not like an ordinary camera. It does not take pictures at a distance. Most Kirlian pictures are of someone's hand which is laid across a plate with a photo sensitive material below it and covered with a dark cloth enclosing the hand and the plate. A very high voltage is then passed through the plate and what is recorded on the photo sensitive plate is the hand and the vital body associated with the hand. So you can see that only small areas of a person or small objects are the only things that may be photographed. In fact, the most famous Kirlian photograph is of a leaf and I will describe this for you later.

Chapter 5

The Kirlian photographs revealed several very interesting things:

1. As mentioned, they demonstrated the existence of the vital, or etheric, body: a) Two individuals who were at odds with each other had their hands photographed at the same time and you could actually see their etheric bodies pulling back from each other. b) When two people in love with each other were photographed at the same time, there auras practically melted into one another.
2. Smoking weakened the aura.
3. Drinking alcohol weakened the aura.
4. It was noticed that a healthy person's aura was larger and brighter than an ill persons, and very significantly: THE ILLNESS APPEARED IN THE ETHERIC BODY BEFORE IT SHOWED UP IN THE PHYSICAL BODY! The implications of this provides material for the next chapter.
5. It was noted that the thoughts of the individual affected the vital body. When an individual thought "hate" the vital body weakened; became smaller in size and less bright in radiance. When the same individual thought "love" the vital body expanded and grew brighter.

The famous Kirlian photograph that I referred to earlier is called "The Phantom Leaf." It is a Kirlian picture of a leaf and its aura. Other objects show at least the etheric aura. As we shall see later, the etheric body is actually the super structure upon which the physical world is built. The upper tip of the leaf appears darkened. The leaf appears whole — but — the tip of the leaf had been cut off just before the photo was taken! If a series of photos are taken it will be seen that after a few minutes the tip fades away and eventually disappears.

The phantom leaf demonstrates that the etheric, or vital body, exists independently of its physical counterpart, but the relationship is so strong that if part of the physical is removed, the etheric will eventually disintegrate and disappear. This suggests that when an individual dies, the etheric body continues to live for a short period before disintegrating. But, there is no such thing as "death" anyway.

I like to throw little things like that at you occasionally, just to pique your interest. We will discuss this in detail later on.

CHAPTER SIX
LIVE TO EAT.....EAT TO LIVE

Patient: Doc! Doc! You have to examine me quick.
Doc: But I don't see anything wrong with you.
Patient: I know, Doc. Ain't it wonderful!

Continuing with our discussion of the vital, or etheric body, we mentioned that illness shows up in the etheric before appearing in the physical. The opposite is also true: if healing is taking place it appears first in the etheric.

Illness in the etheric shows up in a couple of different ways. It appears as a weakened aura. The lines of energy are not as big, bright or strong as in a healthy body. The second way that illness shows up is in blockages of the free flow of energy in the etheric body, which appear as darkened areas. Incidentally, a weak aura may also be an indication of poor energy levels in the physical. So if your get up and go got up and went, strengthening your etheric aura may take your get up and gone, and get it going again. What a wonderful diagnostic tool this would be if more were known about the etheric body.

Consider this. Since all illness shows up in the etheric body first, and then appears in the physical body, if you can maintain a healthy etheric body at all times then the physical body should never become ill.

If this is indeed the case, then what we need to do is to find out what is causing any weakness and blockages in your etheric body, and then just don't do those things. I mean if your head keeps hurting because you keep banging it against the wall, and you want the pain to go away, then stop banging your head up against the wall or take the wall away!

We are told from ancient Hindu teachings that the vital body is fed by something called Prana. Prana is an energy that is radiated by the sun and is the life-force that sustains all life on this planet. This life force is seen by clairvoyants as a golden, dancing light, and might appear somewhat like little particles of dust reflecting the light of the sun as it pours through a window of a house. This energy enters the body of man and travels throughout the body, animating the body and giving it life. If, for some reason, there is either not enough Prana entering the body, or it is somehow blocked and not allowed to move freely throughout the body, then a condition of illness or weakness is the result.

There are three ways in which the body receives Prana. The first, and most obvious, is directly from the sun and so it is a good idea to get out into the sunshine as much as you can. Have you ever noticed that during the winter you seem to have a lack of energy? That is because the sun is not bearing directly onto the earth and there is less Prana around.

The second way that we receive Prana is from the air that we breathe. Prana comes from the sun, and as it penetrates the atmosphere, it fills the air. One of the problems here is that many people breathe in a very shallow manner, and therefore do not take in much Prana with each breath. A good, deep breath, is a three part breath. What you do is breathe deeply into your abdomen and when that cavity is filled, continue to breathe into your chest. When that is full, you will find that you can actually draw in a little more air into your back area. It's a great idea to start your day off with several of these deep breaths when you first arise in the morning, either through an open window or by stepping out-of-doors. You may find that you don't need that cup of coffee to get you going in the morning.

For ordinary, every day breathing, abdominal breathing is the healthiest. What I meant earlier when I said that many people's breath is shallow, is that they breathe only into their chest. Check yourself out. Just relax and see where the breath goes. Does it go into the chest or into the abdomen? If into the chest, you should then practice abdominal breathing.

> *I'm reminded of a comic strip that I read years ago. It was about a quaint little animal character named Pogo. Pogo was dealing with the amount of pollution in the air which was becoming a growing concern at that time and probably a greater concern today. Pogo was describing his uncle who went out of doors one morning, took a deep breath and toppled over dead. "You know," said Pogo, "if that man had stopped breathing, he'd still be alive today." Well, polluted air or not, we still have to breathe and we still need to take in that Prana.*

The third, and perhaps the main way that most people get Prana into their system is from the food that we eat. Except that Prana-wise, all foods are not created equal. I'm not going to get on my soap box about your diet, or maybe I am, but most people eat terribly. Their diet seems designed to intake the greatest amount of food with the least amount of Prana, forcing their digestive system to work overtime with the least amount of benefit.

I remember a television commercial in which the man is complaining about an upset system because of the food that he just ate and the wife says, "Don't worry, dear, just take some Bloppo and you'll feel better in a few minutes." Sure enough, the guy takes Bloppo and he is feeling better, whereupon, he says, "Now I can eat some more of this junk that just made me sick because I can take some more Bloppo and feel better." Does the logic of this strike you the way it does me? Where is the wife who says, "If you want to feel better, dear, stop eating that horrible food?" And do you really think that Bloppo has eliminated all the damage done by that food? This kind of screwball logic is also illustrated by the following story:

> *A scientist is experimenting with fleas. He has taught the flea to jump over a string on command. He then proceeds to remove the four legs of the flea, one at a time, commanding the flea to jump each time. He removes one leg, commands the flea to jump and the flea jumps. He removes the second and third with the same command and each time the flea jumps. Then he removes the flea's last leg and commands it to jump, but the flea just stays there. The scientist concludes, therefore, that when you remove all of the legs of a flea, it goes deaf!*

What you eat matters! Some foods will enliven you, and some foods will poison you. If you keep eating foods that contain no Prana, your etheric body is going to become ill and so will your physical body. Of course, there is a direct correlation between the atoms of the physical body and the "atoms" of the etheric body, and if you consume foods that are damaging to the physical body this will cause disruptions in the etheric body, which will in turn causes illness in the physical body that are sometimes severe and even life threatening.

When you are young, it seems that you can eat anything with impunity and your body still functions very well. That's one of the blessings of youth, and, if you are young, you may think that what I am saying is not for you. But it is. It catches up with you. Ask the people that you know aged forty or fifty and see what they have to say. The worst part is that people have been conditioned to believe that they are supposed to get sick and slow down when they reach that age, but it's just not true! Treat your body right and you should continue to be healthy and feel good way past your fifties. You need the Prana and you need to stop eating the stuff that is making the Bloppo company rich. What is even worster (to coin a word) is that these people do not make the connection of how they feel with what they eat and they continue on the same poor diet that made them sick in the first place!

Let's face it. If Prana comes from the sun, then the foods that are most exposed to the sun are going to have the greatest amount of Prana. You got it, folks; fruits and vegetables. Cows eat grass. Plenty of Prana there. If you eat cows, you're getting second hand Prana and not much of it. Do you want to know what eating cows does for your body? Look up John Robbins book or video, "Diet for a New America." It's not a pretty picture and it is environmentally insane.

I could write a whole book on the subject, but I did write a booklet dealing with proper diet. At this point, you might even be thinking, "What has any of this to do with Metaphysics and Spirituality?" Well, it does. The food we eat has a major impact on our body, mind, and spirit. Metaphysically, spirit needs a pure body to manifest through, but we will talk more about that later.

Right now, I'd like to give you some simple do's and don'ts about what to eat and what not to eat:

- Do eat lots of fruits and vegetables, but not at the same time. Fruit should be eaten separately, because of it's quickness of digestion, to avoid having it putrefy in your system and cause you acid stomach or heartburn. Sound familiar? Fruit in between meals; a half hour before eating anything else.
- Vegetables should include a lot of green leafies. I think Edgar Cayce's formula was two or three vegetables above the ground to one below.
- Do drink at least eight glasses of water a day. That's water, I said.
- Do use extra virgin Olive Oil with your salads.

I'm afraid the don'ts far outweigh the do's and you're probably not going to like this list:

- Don't eat beef or pork. Takes forever to digest and provides very little Prana. Also lots of uric acid as these animals are slaughtered under very fearful conditions.
- Don't eat fried foods
- Don't intake caffeine in any form: coffee, tea, soda.
- Don't eat sugar, or sugar substitutes, which are even worse for you.
- No dairy products, though goats milk or goats milk cheese are okay. They are a lot easier to digest.
- No white flours. Bread, pasta, rice, etc.

Does this mean that I want you to be a vegetarian? Not exactly, though it wouldn't be a bad idea. Fish and fowl are alright to eat. They are a lot easier to digest. I'm not really suggesting that you change your diet radically. I want to make you aware that there is probably some improvement that most of you can make in your eating habits, and, you can get on the right track by adding one good thing to your diet and taking away one bad thing, then I will have at least helped you move in the right direction.

- Oh, yes, if you are a smoker, please do yourself and the world a great favor and stop right now! You just don't know what damage you are doing to yourself, physically and spiritually.
- Drinking alcohol is almost as bad.

Okay. I'm off my soap box. I hope I'm stepping off of my own free will and not because somebody pushed me off. Socrates said, "I do not live to eat. I eat to live." I would say that is a word from the wise.

CHAPTER SEVEN
HYLOZOISM

I am you and you are me and we are all together. I am the egg man. I am the walrus. Goo goo ga joob."
- The Beatles
All for one and one for all - Dumas
[and all are one - me]

Hylozoism is an actual word that has an actual meaning. It is important to understand that meaning because a lot of what follows in this book will make reference to it.   It is the theory that there is no such thing as dead matter. In other words, everything is alive.

I have developed a kind of "proof" that this is so. You will recall way back in the introduction of this book that I said we would begin with just one premise: that there is an Infinite, Omnipresent, Omniscient Being that we call the Creator, God, etc. If this is so, and we accept that this to be so, because that is our initial premise. If you will indulge me, I am going to do the impossible. I will circumscribe infinity and ask you to use your imagination in accepting that this circle represents all that there is — Infinity.

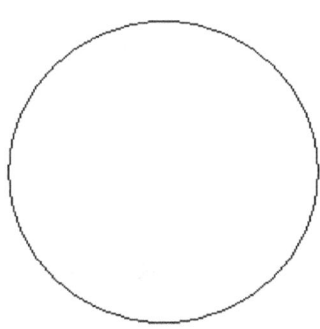

There it is—the Infinite, the All, the There-is-Nothing-Else. Now visualize a time before time existed. A time before space existed. A time when nothing existed except this Great Being. And this Great Being began to think, and for this Great Being to think, was, for Him, to Create. What He thought came into Being, and in His Mind He pictured the vast Universe. And, as He thought about it, it began to form. After what we would consider long periods of time (of course time did not exist yet) the galaxies, the suns, the planets, the moons, the asteroids, and all that there is, appeared, as did life forms of all kinds, and this Creation was sustained until the present day.

And now for the $64,000,000,000,000,000,000 question: Out of what materials did the Creator create the Universe? Here, we have two symbols for infinity:

Does this imply that the Creator took the material from one of these infinities for use in the other infinity? Not possible, you say? I agree. Infinite is infinite, and it must include all. There could not be two infinities. Therefore, there is only one place that this Infinite Being could have gotten the resources used to create the Universe, and that was from within Himself, because there was nothing else! The totality of vibrational energy that defines the Universe was originally described by the great patriarch, Abraham, as the Living God. Everything and everyone in the universe exists in the image of God. There also cannot be anything that is not part of God, because — you guessed it — God is Infinite! Therefore, everything has to be alive, because it is all part of God.

So you see, one of these infinities has got to go. Erase it. It doesn't exist. Let me give you a little equation here:

God=Life=Energy=Vibration

To repeat — Everything is God, therefore everything is alive. Everything is in motion (vibrating) and all vibration is Divine energy. There is only one thing missing from this equation. It is missing because it is an intangible factor. All is Life and all is Vibrating, but not all is vibrating at the same rate and not all is of the same consciousness. It has been said in the ancient writings that nothing exists except vibration and consciousness. You may want to refer back to the discussion on the Real and the Unreal in Chapter four.

Look at the Beatle lyrics again. If the whole universe is actually part of God, albeit at differing rates of vibration, then we are all part of that Great Being and "I am you and you are me and we are altogether. I am the Egg man, I am the Walrus (or the Carpenter or the Gopher, or whatever) goo goo ga joob." The mysterious "goo goo ga joob" are just nonsense syllables that mean "How about that!"

We're all One. We're all part of this Great Being. There is nothing else, and therein lies the true Brotherhood of Man. Wonder not if you are your brother's keeper. You are. We are all One in God and God is One within each of us, and any apparent separation defines the Illusion that is spoken of in the East! Not that again? I'm afraid so. That's the way it is. When Jesus said to "love your neighbor as yourself," he could have added, "because your neighbor is yourself." Well, goo goo ga joob!

Take some time to review Hylozoism again while I leave you with this story:

The zoo keeper is outside the cage of a large ape and he looks in and wonders, "Am I my brother's keeper?"
The ape looks out from inside the cage and wonders, "Am I my keepers brother?"

CHAPTER EIGHT
WHAT'S GOING ON HERE?

Truth is stranger than fiction
-Robert Ripley ("Believe it or not")

    The idea here is to connect all the dots with four straight lines without removing the pencil from the paper (solution to follow).

•   •   •

•   •   •

•   •   •

- Case #1) A group of people go to a place in northern Scotland and plant these magnificent gardens in soil so sandy and climate so prohibitive that only the sparsest and the hardiest of grasses can grow. From these gardens they produce eighty pound cabbages, forty pound tomatoes, and flowering plants eight feet tall!

- Case #2) A man sends a thought two and a half miles to a plant. The plant is hooked up to a polygraph which, in turn, is hooked up to a switch wired to the engine of a car. The instant that the thought is projected, the switch is thrown and the engine of the car starts up! (I wish my car started that well.)

- Case #3) A man with no medical training lies down and puts himself into a self induced trance and answers health questions about individuals whom he has never met. In many cases, they are hundreds of miles away. The resulting information is so helpful and accurate that a 90% healing rate results, even in cases that were given up as hopeless by medical doctors!

Chapter 8

I am sure that there are still some people alive somewhere on this planet who do not believe that the so-called "psychic phenomena" or the "paranormal" exist anywhere but in the imagination (or hallucination) of someone's overactive mind. But I believe that most people recognize that there are happenings in this world that scientists would call "unexplained phenomena" or "psychic phenomena." Most of us are aware that even our law enforcement institutions have called in psychics to help to solve crimes where they have reached a dead end in their investigations. Many people that I've spoken to have either had experiences themselves of a psychic nature or know of someone who has. We've all heard stories of people who for various reasons were prevented from being aboard a particular flight, ship, car, bus, or train, only to find out later that there had been an unfortunate accident and that person was thereby miraculously saved. Stories abound of people who were either saved from tragedy, or led to the rescue of someone else through premonition, hearing a cry for help, or even hearing voices in their head telling them where to look. There are many stories of encounters with angels.

Most of these stories are anecdotal and not very well documented, so they can easily be dismissed by the scientific community. I would like to present to you with the three cases listed at the opening of this chapter. They are all well documented and witnessed by many. For that reason, one would expect them to be thoroughly investigated; not to find out if they occurred, because we know that they did occur, but rather, how and why they occurred. It may be difficult to bring some of these phenomena into a controlled laboratory setting for further study, but when confronted with well-documented extreme cases, such as these, the scientist will often play "ostrich," hiding their head in the sand by refusing to acknowledge the possibility that anything exists beyond the physical, exoteric world. It is apparent to this author that these three cases, like many others, should have received substantially more investigation. Remember Albert Einstein: "Condemnation without investigation is the height of ignorance."

I know that at this point it appears that I am really down on the scientific community. But, that is not totally true. I have great respect and admiration for them as they work within their own specialized fields of investigation. My quarrel is with the narrow confines that they have constructed for themselves, often failing to grasp the "big picture" because of their inability to think "out of the box" — the exoteric box.

This would be the appropriate place to give you the four line solution to the nine dots:

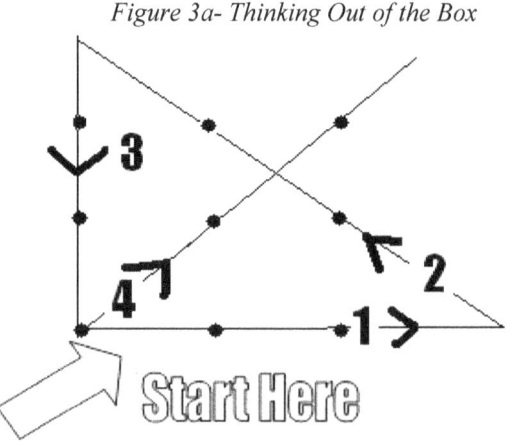

Figure 3a- Thinking Out of the Box

In order to do this, you have to go outside the box that the dots seem to create. Keep yourself in the box and you always come up a little bit short. I suppose that it is a dotty kind of puzzle, but it does illustrate the point. It's kind of like Plato's story of the cave people who are chained together with their backs to the light and all they can see is their shadows on the wall and those two dimensional figures represent their reality. If we continue to think in the typical three or four dimensional manner (with time as the fourth dimension), then the seeming impossibility of what I'm about to describe to you, is indeed impossible. We've got to get out of our exoteric box and explore the possibilities within the multi-dimensional esoteric world recently hypothesized by cutting edge physicists.

Chapter 8

Figure 3b- Thinking Out of the Box

The Three Cases

Case # 1: Findhorn

In 1962, a group of people headed by Peter and Eileen Caddy went to Findhorn, Scotland, to establish a spiritual community, led there by information "channeled" through Eileen (more on channeling later). What happened there is a remarkable and incredible story, which you can read about in detail in "The Magic of Findhorn" by Paul Hawken, published by Harper & Row and "The Spirit of Findhorn" by Eileen Caddy, also published by Harper & Row.

Findhorn is located in the north of Scotland near the arctic circle just off the North Sea. The soil is sandy beach capable of supporting only the sparse growth of gorse bushes and spiky grass. In that location, in those prohibitive weather conditions, the Caddy's planted gardens that were so fertile that they produced eighty pound cabbages (yes, you read correctly, 80 pounds), eight foot delphiniums, roses that bloomed in the snow, as well as many other varieties of flowers and other huge vegetables, forty pound tomatoes, and the like.

How did they do it? Did they develop a fantastic new fertilizer? Did they have a machine that turned rough sand into incredibly fertile soil? Did they have huge greenhouses that captured the feeble rays of the sun and magnified them? The answer is "none of the above." Exoteric, inside the box thinking will lead to all sorts of wild guesses and conjectures, but the truth lies outside the boxes, in the esoteric world.

Many thousands of people have visited the Findhorn Gardens in the intervening years and witnessed these remarkable growths; This is no hoax. The Gardens still exist, though not exactly as they were in the beginning.

Chapter 8

Figure 4 - The Magic of Findhorn

Case #2: Cleve Backster

Cleve Backster, one of the country's foremost polygraph experts did some experiments with plants that culminated with Cleve sending a thought back to a plant from a distance of two, or three miles, that was hooked up to a polygraph that was hooked up to a switch which started the engine of his car. You can read about Cleve in the book, "The Secret Life of Plants" written by Peter Tompkins and Christopher Bird, Avon Books, but I heard this account from two separate sources. Two different individuals who had witnessed Cleve's experiments. I guess you could still call this hearsay; they said it and I heard it (that's a pun — just trying to keep you on your toes.)

It all started when Cleve (remember, he's a polygraph expert) was wondering how long it would take moisture to go from the roots of his plant to the leaves, so he hooked up the polygraph to the leaves and much to his surprise, he started to get a readout on the polygraph that looked very much like that of a human being at rest. Wondering if the plant would react like a human if threatened or startled, he made as if to tear a leaf from the plant and the needle jumped. It reacted just as a human would under the same circumstances.

After many experiments, Cleve found out that the plant would react to the thought of destruction as well as the actual threat. An interesting fact here is that the plant seemed to learn and after realizing that no harm was going to befall it, the plant stopped reacting to these fake threats and remained calm.

Cleve also found that the plant reacted whenever anything live was destroyed in its presence. He dropped brine shrimp (little live shrimp used by fisher persons) into boiling water and the needle jumped every time he did this.

Another interesting experiment that Backster performed was to have six people draw slips of paper from a hat. One of these slips of paper designated the individual that picked it to be "the murderer." No one knew who had chosen this slip and the "murder" was committed to secrecy. The "murderer" was to destroy a plant witnessed only by a second plant hooked up to a polygraph. Backster was able to identify "the murderer" because every time this individual entered the room with the plant, the plant reacted and the needle jumped.

Backster performed many other interesting experiments culminating in the dramatic starting of the car from a distance. These experiments have been duplicated by others and their reports corroborated Backster's findings.

Case #3: Edgar Cayce

Edgar Cayce has been called the "Sleeping Prophet" by author Jess Stearn in his very fine book of the same name. There is a wonderful biography of Edgar Cayce written by Thomas Sugrue called "There is a River." If you want to get a good feel for the work that Cayce has done, these two books are a good starting point. Cayce wrote nothing himself, but many books have been written based on the information that came from his "readings" as they are called.

There are fourteen thousand of these readings that were given by Cayce over a period of about forty years, up until the date of his death in 1945. These readings were all transcribed and can be read word for word at the A.R.E. Foundation located in Virginia Beach, Va.. A.R.E. stands for the Association for Research and Enlightenment, and it was started to preserve and disseminate the extensive teachings and wisdom found in Cayce's readings. The original buildings also housed a healing clinic, and Cayce had dreams of building a hospital based on the healing information that came across in his readings. Almost all of the treatments suggested were based on natural healing principles and did not involve drugs and chemicals.

Most of the readings were given over considerable distance for people that Cayce would never meet. Most were desperate people that had received no help from the orthodox medical community. People would write to Cayce with questions which were presented to Cayce as he lay in a self-induced trance and this man, who had no medical training, would suggest treatments that were ninety percent effective in producing healing. The feeling is that the percentage would have been even higher if all of the instructions given in the readings had been followed exactly, but this was not always the case. I don't know if that figure of ninety percent has sunk in yet. Ask your doctor what his percentage of effectiveness is, especially with what we would call "hopeless cases".

The question is: how could a man lying in a trance in Virginia Beach seem to be examining the body of a man living somewhere in Indiana, lets say, and speak as if he were present in Indiana examining the body while all the while still lying there back in Virginia Beach? How could he be in two places at the same time?

There are recorded instances where Cayce actually remarked about conditions in the home of the individual that was receiving the reading. Remarks like, "What a cheery pair of striped pajamas you are wearing" — or — "What lovely flowers those are," can be found in the transcriptions of the readings.

Cayce did what he did. There is no denying it. There is no claiming that it is a hoax, though he received plenty of flack while he was alive. It's all there. It's all documented. Follow-ups on many cases have also been documented. The question is; why is nobody doing serious research to discover how Cayce accomplished what he did? It's not good enough to say that he was unique, or different and let it go at that. Just because the answers are not to be found in the exoteric world does not mean that it is not worthy of study. As long as the scientific community keeps playing ostrich, we are going to have to keep searching for answers in the esoteric world.

There are a couple of other interesting things worthy of note: in many of the so-called "health readings" Cayce would refer to the "past lives" of the individual in order to explain why they were having difficulty in their current life (but, much more on reincarnation later on). The other point is: in over fourteen thousand readings given over a period of forty years, Cayce never contradicted himself! Think about that. Can you go a month without contradicting yourself? A week? A day? How about five minutes? It's really quite remarkable.

On a personal note, if not for Edgar Cayce's work, my beloved wife, Anita, would not be alive today. She was slowly dying, a good number of years ago, and was receiving no help from the doctors. Cayce, of course, was no longer alive, but we read about Castor Oil packs in the Jesse Stearn book, The Sleeping Prophet. Castor Oil packs had been recommended in many of the readings and we decided to try them since nothing else had helped. After taking just one Castor Oil pack she started to show an improvement and because of that we were able to pursue those natural forms of healing that led to her complete recovery. But, that's a long story for another time.

CHAPTER NINE
WHAT'S REALLY GOING ON HERE?

Anyone who thinks he has all the answers just hasn't learned to ask the right questions - Albert Einstein.

There was this lion who went roaring through the jungle at every animal that crossed his path, "Who's the King of the Jungle?" and all the animals said, "Oh, you are, mighty lion," and the lion would reply, "That's right and don't you forget it." He continued on his way, roaring at monkeys, giraffes, leopards, and so on, until he came across an Elephant. He roared at the Elephant, "Who's the King of the Jungle?" The Elephant shrugged his shoulders, picked up the lion in his trunk, spun him around a few times and slammed him into a tree. Bruised and battered, the lion looked up at the Elephant and said, "Gee, you didn't have to get so mad just because you didn't know the answer."

Before we can provide esoteric explanations for the three cases cited in the previous chapter, we'll need to get back to some of the heavy stuff and pick up with our discussion of Hylozoism — you remember good old Hylozoism — which states: everything is alive because it is all made from the vibratory substance of the Infinite Being that we call God.

The question is (and hopefully we are asking the right questions, though I don't pretend to have all of the answers), "How did He do it?" If He is this great Infinite Being who transcends all notions of speed, and even Time itself. How is it that we live in a world where most vibrations occur at a much slower rate? In fact, we live in a world where most of the vibrations that define the physical plane can be measured. For example, we know that sound energy exists within a certain range of frequencies and wavelengths, as do radio waves, x-rays, visible light, and so on.

The answer lies within the question. God took a portion of His infinite vibratory energy and slowed it down. And, as these vibrations slowed down, they formed "planes," which you might think of as different octaves of vibration. These "octaves" then descended through seven planes, the lowest of which we call the physical plane: the plane of the exoteric world. Now, each one of these planes has seven sub-planes, so our metaphor of seven musical octaves holds true.

The Bhagavad Gita says, Krishna speaking, "Having pervaded the world with a fraction of myself, I yet remain." Krishna, represented God in the Bhagavad Gita. From this statement we are led to believe that this manifested universe is but a fraction of this Infinite Being.

Please realize that much of what is being presented in this book is a simplification of what has been generally referred to as Cosmo-Genesis, as described in "The Secret Doctrine" by H.P. Blavatsky, founder of the Theosophical Society. The Secret Doctrine is a monumental late 19th century work, representing the first presentation of Eastern philosophy to the Western world. It has been called the "Ageless Wisdom." This work is long and quite difficult and is not recommended to the beginning student. Much of the same information can also be found in the Alice Bailey books, dictated to Alice Bailey by the Master Djhwal Khul from "the other side of the curtain." (We will also discuss "Masters," or so-called "Ascended Beings," in a later chapter).

You see, we've definitely moved into the esoteric world, so, by definition, it is difficult to prove much of what I am telling you now. If you are looking for empirical proof, that exists only in the exoteric world, and, thanks to "people of great vision" we have gone well beyond that. As with any scientific hypothesis, however, we state our principles and axioms, and proceed logically, reasoning from initial assumptions, and we follow this logic to "wherever it leads." That is our basic methodology.

Perhaps the most obvious demonstration of how God "slows down" vibrations to increase density can be found in the creation and sustenance of the element water: H_2O. If water is heated, it's vibrations speed up, and it becomes steam; if made cooler, the vibrations slow down and it becomes ice. One substance — three conditions.[1] Think of God as One substance manifesting in seven conditions.

These seven planes are named :

> 7) The Divine Plane
> 6) The Monadic Plane
> 5) The Atmic Plane
> 4) The Buddhic Plane
> 3) The Manasic, or Mental Plane
> 2) The Astral, or Emotional Plane
> 1) The Physical Plane

They are usually represented like this:

> DIVINE
> MONADIC
> ATMIC
> BUDDHIC
> { HIGHER MANAS
>   LOWER MANAS
> ASTRAL
> PHYSICAL

---

[1] Heat actually transitions matter through four states: solid, liquid, gas, and plasma. Plasma is created by heating gas, which ionizes its electrons. This causes a luminous glow sometimes called "Saint Elmo's Fire" or the "Candles of David."

Chapter 9

Notice that the Manasic, or Mental Plane, is broken into two sections, Higher and Lower. The three lower planes; the Physical, the Astral and the Lower Mental, are referred to as the "lower self," or, the "personality." The three levels above that, the Higher Mental, the Buddhic and the Atmic, are called the "Higher Self", or the "Spiritual Nature."

This study will deal primarily with the lower self, this being the most practical aspects of our selves, and that which we can most easily identify with. It is the Physical Plane where the most can be accomplished to move us along the path of spiritual evolution. In fact, it is perfecting the lower nature that leads us to becoming fully awakened Spiritual Beings. Much, much more on this later.

Each of these planes has seven sub-planes. The Physical Plane and its seven sub-planes are:

> ATOMIC
> SUB-ATOMIC
> SUPER ETHERIC
> ETHERIC
> GASEOUS
> LIQUID
> MINERAL

The thing that must be understood is that the terms "Etheric" and "Atomic," as used here, are not the same terms as those used in exoteric science. Sorry about the confusion, but that's the way it is. The Etheric sub-plane is that which is photographed in Kirlian Photography. The sub-planes above are not measurable at the current time, since there are no instruments capable of measuring vibrational energy that subtle. They are, however, still part of the physical plane.

The question will naturally arise; "What has this to do with humanity?" — or — "What is the purpose of the seven Planes?

As far as we know, these planes were created because God wanted us to have certain experiences with matter within each of these planes so that we might evolve. We are swept up in a grand Plan of Evolution, the ultimate purpose of which is beyond what we are capable of knowing at this time. Furthermore, this Evolution is an Evolution of Consciousness. The evolution that takes place in the physical world is such that the evolving consciousness will have a more refined vehicle to inhabit.

The only way that we can learn from these seven planes is to experience the matter of these planes and the only way that we can experience the matter of these planes is to have a body made of the same matter as the plane which we are to experience! This would seem to imply that we have bodies made of the matter of each one of these planes. But we only have a physical body, don't we? Or do we?

It is reasonable to suggest that if we did not have a physical body, we would not be able to experience the physical world. You would have no eyes to see, no ears to hear, no sense mechanism to touch with, and so on. You would be like a creature totally unaware that this physical world even existed. Similarly, if we did not have an Astral (emotional) body, we would not be able to experience the vibrations that fall within the Astral plane. And, if we did not have a Manasic (mental) body, we would not be able to experience the vibrations of that plane either.

You know that you have emotions. What you may not know is that these emotions are experienced through a body made of emotional matter. This concept is a bit difficult to grasp, because we feel these emotions in our physical body. The reason for this is that there is a correlation between the atoms of the physical body and those of the emotional body. When our emotional body is vibrating strongly, they are felt in the physical body.

Let me repeat. If you did not have a physical body you would not be able to experience the physical world; if you did not have an emotional body, you would not be able to experience the emotional world. We will discuss the Astral Plane and the emotional body in detail later on.

Referring back to the diagram of the Seven Planes: The Divine Being shoots off a large number of spark-like miniatures of Itself. These spark-like miniatures of God are called Monads, and they begin their existence in the Monadic Plane. This is your true essence. In fact, if someone were to ask you what you are, you could truthfully say: "I am a Monad." This Monad then descends through the remaining planes taking on matter of each one, like someone putting on several different coats made of different materials. This Monad (which is you) is now able to experience whatever these planes have to offer, because It (you) has a body made up of the matter of each of these planes.

How come we can't see this inner vibrating essence? First of all, the energy is much too subtle. It is definitely real, and it is definitely matter — but, it is very subtle matter. Look at it this way: if you take a light bulb and apply five or six coats of paint to the outside of it, the filament which was quite visible in the beginning is no longer to be seen. Instead, all you see is the outer coat of paint. The filament would represent the Monad and the outer coat of paint would represent your physical body. It is only the "outer coat" that is visible to the naked eye. Just as the filament of the bulb continues to burn, so does the Monad within you continue to burn.

I told you this was going to be the heavy stuff. Now you can breathe a sigh of relief. This is as heavy as it gets. Now, we are in a position to get further insights into "What is Really Going On Here?"

CHAPTER TEN
WHAT'S REALLY GOING ON HERE?

Sign Over the Entrance to the Skeptics Club:
Don't confuse me with the facts, my mind is made up!
Conversations overheard at the Skeptics Club:
When I see it, I'll believe it.
When I believe it, then I'll see it.
I may see it, but I won't believe it.
I may believe I see it, but I still won't believe it.
I may believe that I see it, but I believe that I won't see it.
I may see that I believe it and believe that I see it, but I won't.
I believe that I believe that I see it, but I don't see that I believe it.
I see it, I believe it, I believe it, I see it, but I don't and you better believe it!

Let's review the three cases in Chapter Eight:

Case #1 - The Findhorn Gardens

The people who were led to Findhorn, were directed there by entities using Eileen Caddy as a "channel." "Channeling," as it is called, is contact by an individual of this world by an individual usually existing on the Astral Plane, sometimes the Manasic Plane and very, very rarely, the higher, Spiritual Planes. These individuals from the other planes can sometimes see things more clearly than we can because they are unencumbered by a physical body. I must caution you here that this is not always the case. The information that comes to us through channels is not necessarily of the same level or quality. This will be dealt with in more depth when we discuss the Astral Plane.

Having arrived at Findhorn, Eileen became aware that there were Nature Spirits, little creatures that worked with the growing of plants, flowers, vegetables, and so on, and these Nature Spirits agreed to assist the Findhorn Community in growing their gardens. The impressive results of this effort were discussed earlier. Impossible flowers and vegetables flourishing in impossible conditions.

Does it sound fantastic? Of course it does, but the explanation fits the facts. Where are these nature spirits? They are all around us, but invisible to most people. Many people who joined the community at Findhorn reported having encounters with these nature spirits. Were they all imagining this? Imagination may be a wonderful thing, but it does not grow forty pound tomatoes.

Case #2 - Cleve Backster

The Cleve Backster experiments were witnessed by many different people and duplicated by several, so the point is not to wonder whether the stories are true or not, but rather, to find a satisfying explanation. More than anything else, his story helps to demonstrate the existence of the Astral and Mental Plane, providing insight into some of the "goings on" within these planes.

Several things were observed: first, the plant(s) used in his experiments showed signs of behavior very similar to a human being on an emotional level. Second, the plant(s) responded to thoughts projected toward it, demonstrating a form of telepathy. Third, on a rudimentary level, the plant seemed to learn and retain some memory, as in the ability to identify "the murderer".

To attempt to explain all of these happenings in exoteric terms would almost certainly be doomed to failure. Esoterically, we understand that all life is evolving and has some form of consciousness depending on what rung of the evolutionary ladder they happen to be on. Let me explain further. If we view all things as being alive (Hylozoism), and all are part of God (no other possibility), then all that exists has consciousness at some level because it is all made of God stuff. The consciousness of physical matter, for example, is demonstrated by the fact that minerals will always respond the same under the same given conditions. If this were not so, all of the scientific progress made in chemistry to codify the Periodic Table of Elements would not have been possible. So, we might say that the inherent natural properties of these elements describes its level of consciousness. Consciousness in the mineral world therefore looks very different than human consciousness. Just because the consciousness of minerals is not easily observable does not mean that it is not there.

The vegetable kingdom is on the next rung of the evolutionary ladder above the mineral kingdom, followed by the animal kingdom and the human kingdom. Humans may exist within this Infinite Being, but for us to presume that the human kingdom is the end-all-be-all of evolution would be very presumptuous indeed. It would be reasonable to assume that there are kingdoms beyond the four just mentioned.

Getting back to the vegetable kingdom, our observations of Cleve Backster and his experiments suggests that the vegetable kingdom possesses a very rudimentary Astral (emotional) and Manasic (mental) body. This is not as far-fetched as it may seem. We know that animals and humans possess these bodies by observing their behavior, so, if we observe this behavior in the vegetable kingdom, then why should we not come to the same conclusion?

Remember, we are not attempting to establish whether Backster did what he did, or not. We know that he did. We are trying to understand how what happened happens. Are our observations conclusive? No, but once again this is a reasonable explanation of the facts.

Case #3- Edgar Cayce

One cannot say too much about the work of Edgar Cayce, undoubtedly one of the greatest psychics and humanitarians that ever lived. Cayce devoted his time and his talents to helping others. Once asked if he had one prayer to help him live his life what would it be. He replied, "Others, Lord, others."

Chapter 10

Once again, we are not in the position of establishing if Cayce did what he did, but rather, how he did it. The records are clear. As remarkable as his accomplishments were, they are absolutely true and indisputably so. Earlier, I posed the question: "How could Edgar Cayce seem to be in two places at the same time when he was, in fact, lying in trance in one place while making comments about an individual that he was examining miles away, and giving medical advice when he had no medical training!

For the esoteric explanation of that, we have to examine some of the conditions that exist in the Astral and Mental Planes. Time and space are manifestations of the physical plane. In the Astral and Mental planes time and space do not exist in the same way. In fact, there has been much recent scientific speculation about the existence of more dimensions than the four that we are so familiar with: length, width, depth, and time. For example, picture yourself standing in the doorway of a classroom. From your vantage point you can see into the room and you can also see what is going on out in the hallway so that you can relay these events back to the people in the classroom. You seem to be in two places at the same time. This is similar to what happens in the Astral and Mental Plane. It is as if Cayce were standing in the doorway between these two points and it doesn't matter what the physical plane distance might be, for in the other planes, time and space do not exist in the same manner.

As to the medical information given by Cayce, it must seem obvious that it did not come from Cayce himself but from individuals that did possess this medical knowledge and furthermore were familiar with the workings of the etheric body and were able to see and analyze this body and give recommendations for bringing about a condition of health in the Vital body which was then reflected as a healing in the physical body.

In his trance state, these individuals were able to communicate with Cayce and Cayce was able to relay the information to those that were recording it. Who these entities were is another question. They were apparently living in the Astral or Mental plane and from that plane were able to contact Cayce through his Mental body and from his Mental body, Cayce, being in a physical body, was able to then relate what he was being told. How these other individuals came to be dwelling on the Astral and Mental planes must be saved for a later discussion. Incidentally, the reason that I keep referring to individuals (plural) is that it is believed that there was actually a medical team that worked through Cayce. Cayce began every reading with, "Yes, we have the body," and closed with, "We are through for the present."

As far as the information about past lives, Cayce sometimes described being led to the "Akashic Record," which might be thought of as God's memory for all that has happened since the beginning of time. Cayce was then able to "read" the book containing the information about the individual that he was giving the reading for and was able to review the past lives of that individual as they appeared in the Record.

Once again, the explanation given here is reasonable when one accepts the existence of these inner planes. Right now we are still working on assumptions and theory. That is not necessarily a bad place to be. The Molecular Theory also started out as theory, but it explained so many things, that it came to be widely accepted even before it could be proven. If we can also reasonably demonstrate the existence of these inner planes by bringing them to bear on conditions that we can observe in our own lives, then perhaps we can accept it even before it becomes established with exoteric certainty. At least, the existence of these planes provides us with a plausible explanation for the three cases stated above.

CHAPTER ELEVEN
TELL ME, CAN YOU FEEL IT?

Conversations overheard at the Feels Right Club:
When I feel it, I'll know it.
When I know it, then I'll feel it.
When I feel that I feel it, then I'll know it.
When I know that I know it, then I'll feel it.
When I know that I feel it and feel that I know it, I'll know it.
When I feel that I feel that I know it,
    then I know that I know I'll feel it.
I feel it, I know it, I know it, I feel it, but do I know the
    feeling of knowing I feel it?

The Astral Plane is the Plane of Emotion. Our emotions are housed in our Astral body. When the Astral body vibrates it causes a reaction in the physical body which we interpret as a particular emotion. Feelings of joy, anger, pleasure, despair, etc., are examples of emotions occurring at different rates of vibration. As indicated earlier, you would not be able to experience the Physical Plane without a physical body and you would not be able to experience the Astral Plane without an astral, or emotional, body.

The Astral Plane has seven sub-planes just as the Physical Plane does, but they are not so easily defined, since the Astral body is in constant motion. What we can say about them is that the lower emotions are found on the lower planes and the higher emotions are found on the higher planes. If you think about it, why are they called "lower" and "higher" in the first place? As we shall see shortly, there are many other expressions of the Astral world that have made their way into our every day conversation.

You might ask, "Why are we not able to see this astral body?" The reason you can't see the astral body is because the vibrations are much too subtle and high in frequency. But, there are individuals who have developed astral vision, and thus, they are able to see it. What they are seeing is often described as seeing someone's "aura." The human aura is made up of the etheric vehicle (or body), the astral vehicle and the mental vehicle. People who see auras generally see the astral body, because it is the astral body that contains the most pronounced colors. There are a few who might be able to see the mental body, but that body is much more subtle and its colors are much more delicate and pastel in nature.

Members of the "skeptic's club" will claim that there is no such thing as an aura. To that, we can only say, "If the aura does not exist, then thousands of people over thousands of years in different parts of the world have all had the same hallucination, because they all describe seeing the same thing under similar conditions."

For example, if an individual becomes angry, the description of the aura is that it is an angry looking red. Many of these "visions" have found their way into our every day language, for example: red with anger; green with envy; gray with depression; feeling blue; a yellow streak down one's spine; seeing the world through rose-colored glasses, etc.. This is the appearance of the astral aura under those conditions that have been seen and described by different clairvoyants at many different times in many different places — always the same! So, it is logical to assume that either all of these people are having the same hallucination, or they are seeing what actually exists, and they are describing what they see.

Astral vibrations can become so strong that they can often be felt in a room after people have seriously argued. Everything may seem calm and peaceful, but those who are more atuned can sense that an argument has just taken place by feeling the astral vibrations that are still in the room, causing our own astral bodies to vibrate sympathetically.

Chapter 11

An interesting phenomenon takes place when people are in close proximity to each other. The astral body is larger in size than the physical body and may extend two or three feet beyond it, so your astral body might be intermingling with that of another individual and some of what they are feeling can cause your astral body to vibrate at the same rate. This is most noticeable when the other individual is having a strong feeling, such as depression. You are feeling fine. You come in contact with this aura of depression and all of a sudden you feel "down." (There's another borrowed phrase: "feeling down" = lower vibrations: "feeling up" = higher vibrations). "...and, he walks away feeling as 'happy as a lark.'" This can occur as our aura passes through that of another, perhaps as we pass them on the street. You affect people by the way you are feeling, and they in turn, affect you. It works with both lower and higher emotions, so that if you contact an individual that is particularly "up" you too can become "uplifted."

An individual who can see auras will describe certain colors that are predominant in your aura. If you are a particularly angry person, there will be a lot of crimson red. If you are intellectual, there will be a clear yellow. (The yellow of the "yellow streak down his spine" has a muddier hue, as do all the lower emotions). If you are a loving person, then your aura will show a lot of rose color; a healer will show a nice emerald green, and so on. Notice that hospitals feature a lot of green, including green walls and green clothing. This was not always so, but at some point it was discovered that green provided a more supportive environment for healing.

How do these particular colors show up in your aura? The answer to that is rather interesting. Picture yourself being born with an astral body that is perfectly clear, like a clear beaker of water. (This is not actually so, but let's work with it, because the basic principle is correct). Situations that occur in your life result in your astral body vibrating to different emotions: anger, love, jealousy, compassion, envy, depression, or whatever. For this example, we'll use anger, because we've all experienced anger, and it's easy to relate to. The basic principle, however, holds true for all emotions.

So, here you are, this clear beaker of water, and all of a sudden you become angry. Your astral body vibrates to the frequency of anger and it appears full of lightning bolts of red (since that's what anger looks like). The anger subsides, but it does not completely disappear, the faintest tinge of red remains in the aura. So faint, that it is not really perceptible. If this occurs frequently, another tinge of red is left behind each time, and more and more red gets added to your aura — the red of anger. What does this mean in practical terms? It means that because there is the frequency of the vibration of anger present in your aura that you will tend to anger easily. This becomes a vicious cycle because every time you anger, you deposit more of that vibration in your aura, which then causes you to anger more easily. You become one of those people that "flies off the handle" for what appears to everyone else as no reason whatsoever. I'm not saying that you are one of these people, but we've all met one. An individual who "loses it" at the "drop of a hat." Aren't cliches fun?

This concept is an extremely important one. It helps you to understand some of the reasons that people behave the way that they do. It also gives you a clue as to how you can go about making positive changes in your own behavior. If you can identify an emotion of a lower nature within yourself, one that you would rather live without, you can gradually eliminate that vibration in two ways:

First, because you know how the process works, when you feel this undesirable emotion coming on, do not indulge it. In other words, observe what is happening and decide that you would rather not do that.

The key word here is "observe." You must become the "Observer." I will talk more about being "the Observer" in just a moment. If you do not observe what is happening, your emotions will run through the entire emotional gamut, but you will only realize your experiences after the fact. Too late! The astral body has already vibrated, depositing another tinge of that particular color into your aura. You've got to catch it before it gets out of control. You have to be "awake" and not "asleep."

Perhaps this will provide some insight into what Gurdjieff was talking about when he said that most people are asleep most of the time. What he meant was that people are so caught up in the day-to-day, minute-by-minute events of their lives, reacting to whatever comes their way without ever being able to exert any real control over it. Thus, one must become the "Observer."

It is a little difficult to describe what being the Observer means, but once you have experienced it (and, you no doubt have, without realizing it), you will always be able to identify when you enter into that state of consciousness (which is really what it is).

I have devised a simple means of helping you to identify the Observer within yourself. If you just sit quietly for a moment, and attempt to slow or stop your restless, wandering thoughts; what has often been called "the drunken monkey mind," then you should also be aware of a part of your mind that remains conscious and seems to be "observing" this quiet condition that you have achieved. That is the Observer. The Observer simply observes. The Observer is not your conscience, and it is not judgmental. When you achieve this state of consciousness you will realize that you feel more "awake," more keenly alert, and if you can maintain this condition for any length of time, you will be in a position to observe when your emotions start to run away with you.

Being the "Observer" is just being in a higher state of consciousness, or awareness, if you will. In this manner, you can begin to relate to being at different levels of awareness. You know that there are times when you become so engrossed in what you are reading or watching that you become unaware of your surroundings. Someone may even call your name, and you will not respond.

During that period, you are in a lower state of consciousness with respect to what is going on outside yourself. You are effectively "asleep" in relation to your optimal state of mind. Therefore, what you normally call being "awake," is more like being "asleep," when compared to the "wakefulness" of the "Observer."

When you become aware that an undesirable emotion has begun to take hold, you have reached a critical point. You should not repress the emotion by trying to make believe it doesn't exist. And, you should not fight it by saying to yourself, "I will not be angry, I will not be angry!" as this only feeds the vibration. You must observe what is happening and say to yourself, "I realize that this emotion is beginning to take hold, but I, the true I, do not wish to continue in that direction. I choose instead to vibrate to whatever positive emotion is opposite to the negative one being experienced. For example, if it is anger, choose love or peace; if it is depression, choose hope or joy; if it is selfishness, choose giving and sharing. Whatever it is, choose its opposite, since opposite emotional energies won't coexist. I am not suggesting that opposites cannot coexist, but that they cannot exist in the same time and place. In other words, you can't have both light and dark at the same time, in the same place. If there is any light, then it is not totally dark, and if you are in total darkness, then there is no light. Similarly, you cannot love and hate at the same time, or be both peaceful and hostile, since they are mutually exclusive. You get the idea.

A little more about being the Observer. At first, you will probably find it difficult to maintain that state of wakefulness. You may be able to sustain it for only a minute or two, but, if you keep working at it you can extend the time. You will also find yourself "waking up" more often, although sometimes days may go by before you "wake up," and you will realize that you have been "asleep" for some time. When you are in the state of consciousness of the Observer, you will find that you can function more efficiently at whatever task you are doing, still focusing on the task but observing yourself doing it at the same time. It's like being in the audience of a theater watching a play going on even though you are actually one of the players.

How, then, are you going to be the Observer when you need to be, so that you can head off the unwanted emotion, and replace it with a more desirable one? What will happen, if you have it in your mind that this is what you want to do, is that you will begin to wake up any time an undesirable emotion begins to take place, and you will stay awake long enough to make the decision that you would rather not be experiencing that emotion, choosing a more favorable one instead.

You might ask at this point what all this is going to accomplish. To answer that, you need to know a little more about the astral body. The astral, or emotional body, has "x" number of astral "atoms," and inactive vibrations are eliminated from the astral body, and they are replaced by active emotions. So if you should choose not to anger, but to be loving instead, the anger vibrations lessen and the loving vibrations increase. Now when the clairvoyant looks at your aura he (or she) will see the rose color of love, rather than the crimson red of anger.

Back about ten paragraphs ago I said that there are two ways in which to change the vibrations of your astral body from negative to positive. The second way is to simply fill your astral body with positive feelings all day long. Just keep telling yourself what a loving, giving, understanding, compassionate human being you are, and you will fill your astral body with those vibrations which will, in turn, eliminate the negative vibrations from your astral body as described above.

Now I would like to discuss the Mental Body and how your thinking influences your life and affects all the lower bodies; astral, etheric and physical, through a process that we call "Precipitation."

CHAPTER TWELVE
SO! WHAT DO YOU THINK?

Whadda ya know, Joe?
Nothin, whadda you know?
Twice as much.
Oh.

Many, many years ago, when I was attending Brooklyn Technical High School, I was in a forge shop class hammering away at my assignment, surrounded by other students, also hammering away at the same assignment. Furnaces going, bellows going, it was hot and noisy and I was concentrating for all I was worth, doing the best I knew how. My teacher was a huge man, an artist at his trade, a man who was proud of the fact that he had forged every little piece of his pocket watch by hand. So there I was, hammering away as previously noted, oblivious to everything but the task at hand when all of a sudden this booming voice bellowed at me, "If you knew what you were doing, you wouldn't be doing it!" I nearly jumped out of my skin, almost throwing this hot piece of metal in the process.

He was probably right. Whatever it was that I was trying to forge (I think it was a scribe), it was supposed to have one smooth, flat surface, and I think I had created a different plane with each hammer blow. I was not very good at forge shop.

What is the point of the story? There is a message there for most of us, if not all of us. For the most part, if we "knew what we were doing, we wouldn't be doing it!"

Knowing what we are doing is a function of the Mental Body, which contains the mental aspect of our being. At the stage of development that most of mankind has reached, there is little separation between the Astral and the Mental bodies. There is almost no such thing as a pure thought that is not tinged with emotion, and conversely, there is almost no pure emotion that is not associated with some mental concept. If you think about that for a moment I'm sure you will agree that this is so. For example, I could say that one and one is two, but even simple arithmetic might be tinged with the satisfaction of knowing that, "Hey, I know that one and one is two."

A Sanskrit word was invented to describe this condition. It is called *Kama-Manas*, or "Desire-Mind." There is a strong relation that exists between the two bodies, so whenever I think, my Astral body is set into motion, and it vibrates in tandem with whatever concept is going through my head. If I am thinking lofty thoughts, then I am filling my Astral body with high vibrations of a positive nature and I am uplifted. If, on the other hand, I am thinking lower thoughts, then I am filling my Astral body with lower vibrations of a negative nature, and I am pulled down as my Astral body responds to those lower vibrations.

There is something else that happens when we think. We are continuously creating something called thought-forms. Each thought actually calls forth a form that takes on the quality of that thought, and it is colored (literally) by the nature of that thought. Thought-forms of love are colored rose, thought-forms of anger are colored red; green, with envy, and so on. The colors are the same as those that we talked about earlier when discussing the Astral body. This would necessarily be so because of *Kama-Manas* — the close connection between Astral and Mental. The shape of the thought-form demonstrates the quality of the thought, so that negative thoughts are rather unpleasant in appearance with muddy, brackish looking colors, whereas the positive thoughts take on a more pleasant appearance with clear, lovely colors.

Figure 4 - Angry Thought-Form

Chapter 12

There are three classes of thought-form. Each of the three may be a positive influence in your life and the life of others, or conversely, a negative influence. Edgar Cayce said that, "Thoughts are things and can prove to be crimes or miracles in their application." He also notably said that "Mind is the builder." In Metaphysics we say that, "Energy follows thought." There are other relevant quotes, such as: "As a man thinketh in his heart, so he is." First, we'll take a look at the three types of thought-form:

1) When you think about another individual, the thought-form created travels directly to that individual where it will enter their aura and either:

a) hang around in the aura for a period of time and discharge itself into the aura later on, or
b) be accepted immediately into the aura or
c) be reflected back to the sender if there is no resonant vibration present within the aura of the receiver.

The thought that is being sent may be of a positive, uplifting nature or of a negative downgrading nature. Casey therefore suggests that this thought can become a "miracle" if it has a positive nature, or a "crime" if it has a negative nature. This type of thought-form creates a similar vibration within the sender's aura and so the individual thinking the thought is either helping themselves or harming themselves.

2) When you are thinking thoughts about yourself, the resulting thought-form hangs around your aura, and will discharge itself back into your aura when you are in a period of rest. This type of thought-form constitutes the majority of thought-forms, since most people spend a great deal of time thinking about themselves, i.e., their worries, fears, concerns, likes, dislikes, and so on. Thus, we can easily become self-absorbed and live within a cloud of thought-forms.

3) The third type of thought-form contributes to a mass thought-form of the same quality. For example, if you are waiting on line at the super market and the line is being held up for some reason, you may begin to become impatient, but before long you find yourself being excessively impatient. Here is what is happening: There is a mass thought-form of impatience hanging around the checkout counter. It has been built up through the years by people having impatient thoughts while waiting on line. When you have an impatient thought you "tune in" to this thought-form, and it magnifies your impatience until you become more impatient than you normally would. At the same time, your thought of impatience adds to the existing mass thought-form. This becomes a factor in mob panic or general mob behavior. The thought-form built up is so powerful that if you have any of those vibrations within your aura you can be "caught up" in it.

Does this mean that every little thought that passes through your mind has the same force, the same impact on yourself or others? No. It depends on how intense the thought is, how clearly it is visualized, how much emotional energy is put into it, and how many times it is repeated. So it is the thoughts that you are focusing on and giving energy to that are going to have the greatest impact.

Every thought that you have does have an impact upon your aura, to a greater or lesser degree, as explained above. The result is that your aura is colored according to the types of thoughts and feelings that you have, producing an overall vibratory rate that will sympathetically resonate to like vibrations around you. This means that the negative vibrations in your aura will attract negatives, the positive vibrations will attract positives. From a practical perspective, if you want to attract positive things into your life then you need to fill your aura with positive vibrations. Conversely, the more negative vibrations in your aura, the more negative things will be attracted to you.

Chapter 12

People, in general, are unaware of this process, and therefore indulge themselves in thoughts of every nature. There is no conscious attempt to fill the aura with positive vibrations because they are completely unaware of what is happening and their lives "go up and down like a yo-yo" as an acquaintance of mine described his own life. We are inclined to accept what many of us had been told as children: "If you were only thinking it, it doesn't matter." I'm afraid that is another example of: "It's too cold to snow." The fact is that it does matter what you think! It matters a great deal.

Let me repeat: If you want to bring positive things into your life, you must fill your aura with positive vibrations. That means that you have to start thinking consciously; not allowing negative thoughts to wander through your mind. You have to exercise control over your thinking. Control in the sense that you are aware of the thoughts that are going through your mind and when a negative one shows up, you recognize it is there and say to yourself, "I, the true I, do not wish to have this negative thought, I choose instead to have this positive thought. (Here you choose some positive thought, or Affirmation, or Prayer in its place.) We will talk more about Prayer and Affirmation later on. In order to accomplish this, however, you must first become the "Observer." This cannot emphasized enough.

It is most important that you do not attempt to repress the thought or feeling, pretending that it doesn't exist. Acknowledge its existence, and then choose an alternative, as already indicated. You must also be careful not to affirm a negative, such as: "I will not be angry, I will not be angry, I will not be angry!" In this case you are still focusing on anger and introducing that vibration into your aura. The best thing that you can do is to introduce a vibration which is diametrically opposed to anger, such as peace or love. Remember, opposites cannot coexist within you at the same time.

The magnetic quality of your aura will draw the circumstances of your life to you. If you have built up a negative condition in your aura, you are going to attract negative things into your life. These negative things may take on different forms, and can result in accidents, illnesses, or even financial setbacks.

In Chapter Six, we discussed illness in relation to the etheric body, and I suggested that if you could maintain a perfectly healthy etheric body you would never become ill. We talked about *Prana* and its role in maintaining health. This is of course true and valuable, but the main cause of blockages or weaknesses in the etheric body comes from an astral body that is filled with negative vibrations. These negative vibrations cause your astral body to vibrate in a way that disturbs the balance in the etheric body, and it throws that body out of kilter. Remember, there is a direct correspondence between the "atoms" of the mental body, the astral body, the etheric body and the physical body.

All of this comes about through a process that we call "Precipitation." Precipitation takes place from the mental body on down, and you can visualize a process somewhat like rain falling from the skies (the mental body), passing through the intervening distance (the astral body), and eventually landing on the earth (the physio-etheric body).

We do not have to learn <u>how</u> to precipitate. We are precipitating all the time. The energies of our being precipitate vibrational energy that pulses through our various bodies and into the external world in a continuous stream, much like the waters pouring over Niagara Falls. What we have to learn is <u>what</u> to precipitate. Ideally, "the what" should consist of positive, loving and uplifting thoughts. Those are the kinds of vibrations that we want to precipitate into the Universe. Those are the kinds of vibrations that are going to attract positive circumstances into our lives.

Chapter 12

If it seems to you that I have been saying somewhat the same thing over and over again for the last few paragraphs, its because that is what I have been doing. Obviously, I feel this is important. Once you come to a clear understanding of this information you will realize that you are not a victim of life, you are not a puppet on a string, dancing this way and that, always reacting to whatever is coming your way at the moment — you will realize that whatever is befalling you, whether good or bad, has been the result of the vibrations that you have been sending out into the Universe. You are now in control because you understand the process and you can make it work for you.

One of the things that I am trying to do in this book is to present you with some practical tools that you can work with. It will do you no good if you read this book and think, "That was interesting." And then go about living your life in exactly the same way that you have before. Then this all becomes an intellectual exercise and that is not what is intended. I hope you use these tools and see if they work. See if the astral body works the way I say it does. See if creating positive thought-forms will bring positive things into your life. Experience these things so that you will learn, as I have, that everything works just as described. Don't be like the fellow that buys all the materials that he needs to build a house, has them delivered, buys all the necessary tools, sets them out in front of him and then gets himself a chair, sits down and stares at the tools and the materials. His house won't get built — and, neither will yours. Work with the tools. Prove me right or prove me wrong, but you will never know until you have had the experience yourself!

CHAPTER THIRTEEN
LET'S GET TO WORK

The river was flooding. Rescue teams were out searching for individuals who had not reached dry land. A man in a rowboat spotted a gentleman sitting atop his roof. The water had already reached up to his waist. The man in the rowboat cried out: "Get into the boat and I'll take you to dry land." The gentleman responded: "Don't worry about me. God will save me. You go look for someone else that needs your help." So the man in the rowboat paddled away.

A little while later, the gentleman found himself with water up to his chin when a motor boat went by. The man operating the motor boat said, "Come on aboard, I know that I can squeeze one more passenger on." Again the gentleman responded: "Don't be concerned with me. God will provide my safety. You go and help someone else."

A helicopter out searching for stranded people, spotted just the head of the gentleman who was now in water up to his nose. Dropping a rope he yelled down for the gentleman to grab it and be carried to safety, but you know by this time what the gentleman's response was: "God will take care of me. You go and rescue someone else."

Well, in due time, the waters were up over the gentleman's head, and since he couldn't swim, he unfortunately drowned and he found himself at the gates of heaven where he was asked if he had any special request, whereupon he replied, "I must speak with God," and upon having this request granted, the gentleman stood before God and said. 'God, I have been a good man all of my life; pious, loving and giving. I obeyed your commandments, and I would like to know why it was that you let me drown in the flood?" Whereupon God replied: "Hey, I sent you two boats and a helicopter. What more do you want!?"

This story is not intended to suggest that the reader should picture God in some personified state. It is just meant to illustrate the point that God will provide, but you have to do your part if you want God to provide what you would like Him to provide. God will always provide, but you may not always like what is being provided. We live within an Infinite Being. Whatever energy you put out into this Infinite Being, whether it be words, feelings, thoughts, or deeds, becomes the determining factor for the nature and character of that which you will receive. If you don't like what you are getting then you'd better make a concerted effort to change what you are giving out. This spiritual principle can be stated in a more familiar form: "As you give, so shall you receive." This also describes the Eastern notion of Karma, which we will talk more about later. Alright, enough theory. Let's get down to practical application:

1. The As-If Technique - This technique is based on the principle that "Mind is the builder" and that "Energy follows thought." First you identify something in your life that you would like to change for the better — something about yourself that you don't particularly like — perhaps some mannerism, or how you behave in a given circumstance. Let's say that you are a student going to school and your mind freezes up every time you take a test; even though you know the subject quite well, your grades are pretty poor.

Here is how you apply the *As-If Technique* to this situation. Every day, once or twice, or as often as you can, you sit quietly and visualize yourself taking tests. You see yourself receiving the test with great confidence and being quite calm and focused and bringing forth the correct answers to all the questions. See yourself turning in the test paper with the full knowledge that you have done the very best that you are capable of doing and see yourself receiving the test paper back with a big old "A" and encouraging words from the professor, such as "EXCELLENT WORK," written across the top.

In other words, you visualize yourself in the situation As-If you are doing things just exactly the way that you would desire to do them at all times. What will happen, if you practice this visualization often enough, is that the visualization will become the reality. Because you have "Built it in the Mind," it will come to be in your life. The principle that "energy follows thought" will come to pass, as sure as day follows night — but, don't expect positive results overnight. We are working with subtle energies. It takes time for these thought-forms to Precipitate into your being. Please don't tell me, "I tried it once, and it doesn't work." It does work, but you have to be persistent, and give it time to take hold.

The As-If technique can be used in any circumstance that you wish to change. You just have to use your imagination. Here are some further examples: If you want to stop smoking, see yourself going through each and every day with no desire whatsoever to smoke. Someone offers you a cigarette and you say, "No thank you, I don't smoke."

You find yourself becoming irritated and angry while driving in traffic. See yourself being calm and peaceful. You are having a problem with someone at work. This person irritates you, and you, in turn, irritate this person. See yourself interacting with this person in perfect harmony and friendship.

The opportunities for the As-If technique are endless. Professional athletes use this technique to improve their game. They visualize themselves going through every movement with perfection in tennis, gymnastics, basketball, baseball, football, etc. You are reconditioning yourself to perform in the way that you want. This method works in athletics and in life.

This process, is of course, a form of meditation. Don't let that scare you off, because you think that you can't meditate. Everyone can meditate. If you have ever played out a scene in your mind, you can meditate. There will be a whole chapter devoted to meditation later on.

2. The Affirmation Technique - The Affirmation technique is very interesting, because we use this technique all of the time, but, for the most part, we don't realize that we are using it. We affirm things about ourselves all of the time, but, unfortunately, these things are not always positive. For example: "I'm so clumsy, I would trip over a design in the carpet"; or, "I'm not smart enough to do that" (whatever it is.)"; "I never win anything"; "That's the way I am, that's the way I've always been, and that's the way I will always be"; "I can't do that!" (sing, paint, ride a bicycle, etc.). Every time you affirm something negative about yourself, it becomes part of what you are. It's a self-fulfilling prophecy. Of course, you're saying to yourself, "But that's really the way I am. I can't help it, that's just the way it is." So, which comes first, the chicken or the egg? Are you feeling like the guy who went to the psychiatrist complaining of an inferiority complex, and the doctor says, "You haven't got a complex, you're just inferior?" How did you get to be the way you are? Or, if you do affirm positive things about yourself, how did that come about?

I knew a lady who always won the door prize; maybe not every door prize, but her percentage of winning was remarkable. Having observed her winning the door prize on several different occasions, I approached her and asked her if it didn't seem odd to her that she won with such consistency. Her reply was, "Oh yes, I always win." It didn't seem strange to her, because she knew that she was going to win. She affirmed herself as a winner and she won.

The point is, that it doesn't matter how you came to affirm these things about yourself. It may have begun when you were a child at home, being told over and over again how clumsy you were, or it may have been in school with some music teacher saying that you can't sing, that you are a "listener" or that you are just "dumb." What started it all is not important. What is important, is to know that you can change any of these negatives, by affirming positive things about yourself. Don't ever be like the individual in the example above who thinks that they can't change and that's the way they will always be. You can change. It is the basis of all spiritual growth and evolution. We can, and must, make something better of ourselves. Remember, "energy follows thought!"

Just as in the As-lf technique, it will take time for the Affirmation technique to precipitate into your daily life. Be consistent, persevere and understand that you are working with a well established methodology that will bring the desired results. Believe in it, and believe in yourself. Remember, "Mind is the builder!"

Proceed as you would with the As-lf technique, and identify an area of your life that you would like to change for the better. If you feel, for example, that you get too nervous in stressful situations, then affirm, "I am calm, peaceful and totally in control at all times and in all situations." Then take that affirmation and repeat it over and over again, whenever you have the time and whenever you are "awake" enough to think about it.

How you say the affirmation is important. If, for example, you say it, either aloud or to yourself, but you are also thinking: "Yeah. right! Who am I trying to kid?" then there is no way that the affirmation will be effective because your negative thoughts will interfere with the positive ones. It would not be negative, however, to observe that you have not yet become what you are affirming, because this process builds the affirmation into your being a little at a time, and eventually it will become part of who and what you are.

Another example: if you find yourself at a loss for words, and lack confidence in social situations, then say something like, "I am confident in my ability to always say the right thing at the right time in every situation."

Just as with the As-lf technique, the possibilities are endless. The nice thing about the Affirmation technique is that you can do it any time, any where, and for as short or long a period of time as you choose. Obviously, in this case, more is better. We will talk more about affirmations when we talk about following the "Spiritual Path."

Chapter 13

I am offering you tools to work with. Pick them up. Use them. Build your house. (You remember the guy who bought all the materials, had all the tools and then just sat there doing nothing. Don't be like him.) If you don't take action, nothing will happen. Get in the row boat, grab the helicopter rope. Do something! In the following poem, Lord Tennyson suggests how and why we should positively affirm our inner self:

The sun, the moon, the stars, the seas,
   the hills and the plains ----
Are not these, O Soul, the Vision of Him who reigns?

Earth, these solid stars, this weight of body and limb,
Are they not sign and symbol of the division from Him?

Dark is the world to thee: thyself art the reason why:
For is He not all but thou, that hast power to feel "I am I?"

Speak to Him, thou, for He hears,
   and Spirit with Spirit can meet---
Closer is He than breathing, and nearer than hands
   and feet.

- Alfred Lord Tennyson

CHAPTER FOURTEEN
THIS IS IT

Be ye perfect, even as your father in heaven is perfect - Matthew 5.

Q. How do you sculpt an elephant?
A. You get a great big piece of granite, a hammer and a chisel, and you chip away everything that doesn't look like an elephant.

So now we get down to what this is really, really, really all about. Why are we here? What is the purpose of life? Where are we going?

We are here to become "perfect, even as your father in heaven is perfect." That is the purpose of life. We are going to where perfected people go after they have become perfect.

How do you go about doing this? By taking all the information that I have given you about the astral body and how it works; the mental body, thought-forms, precipitation, being the Observer; and by taking all these tools and techniques to start chipping away at everything that is not perfect.

You begin by first identifying what is not perfect about yourself. You don't need to identify everything. Work on one or two things at a time. As you begin to chip away at these imperfections, you will be taking away the lower vibrations from your aura, or more correctly, you will be transmuting the lower vibrations into higher ones. You will be the magical alchemist changing lead into gold, hate into love, selfishness into selflessness, envy and greed into giving and service — gradually turning all your negatives into positives.

Every time you transmute a lower vibration into a higher one, the overall vibratory rate of your aura becomes a higher vibration. Your aura becomes purified as the dross of these lower vibrations that tend to drag you down are transmuted and you are lifted up higher and higher. And, as your aura is filled with these higher vibrations, you will radiate more and more light, and your consciousness will be raised continually higher as the density and darkness of your lower vibrations are eliminated (transmuted), until you become one of the "...just men made perfect who need go out no more" (Hebrews 12.23).

It is a wonderful, magical process. It's called evolution, for there is truly only one evolution, and that is the evolution of consciousness. As the consciousness evolves it requires a finer and finer body to work through and so the evolution in the physical follows the evolution in consciousness. A finer nervous system is needed, a larger brain capacity, and who knows what else will be needed in the future so that this elevated consciousness will be able to fully express itself. As this process continues, there will come a time when the consciousness is so elevated that it can no longer express itself through a physical body, and the physical body will no longer be needed. When it is no longer necessary, the consciousness will express itself through higher vehicles: the Higher Mental, the Buddhic and the Atmic bodies that are associated with the Monad, as mentioned earlier in this book. Ultimately, full Monadic consciousness would be achieved, until the Monad no longer requires even these higher vehicles or bodies.

You see, God has a Plan for humanity, and though we are not privileged to know what this entire Plan is, we can get certain glimpses of it. We can see this grand scheme of Evolution unfolding as we observe that there are beings around us who are more evolved and those around us who are less evolved. Those truly evolved beings stand out as the great men or women of history; they are those who have done much to further the progress of humanity. We can also see those who are less evolved: savages, thieves, murderers, etc. But, all around us, we can see those who have chipped away many of the imperfections, and those who have still much work to do. To evolve towards perfection — that is why we are here! If you are not working on perfecting yourself, you are not doing your job. This is part of God's Plan; this is God's Will.

This earth has been correctly called "Schoolroom Earth." It is here on Schoolroom Earth that we learn the lessons that enable us to "walk the Path" to perfection.

We are all the "Prodigal Son," who is sent out (as a Monad descending through the layers of our being in a process of Involution) and must sink to the lowest depths (of the physical plane) before realizing that we must return to the "Father's House" and begin to walk the path of perfection (Evolution) that will lead us there.

This process has been called "Self-Realization," with the "Self" corresponding to our higher Spiritual nature, or Soul. At this point, we will have developed a conscious awareness that we are, in fact, spiritual beings. As our evolution continues, we will progress to "God realization," consciously knowing that God is One and we are part of that Oneness.

This process is not a short one, nor is it an easy one. And, it is not possible to accomplish this in a single lifetime. But, God in His Infinite Wisdom, has given us the means to accomplish this, namely: "Karma" and "Reincarnation." Guess what the next chapter is going to be about.

CHAPTER FIFTEEN
IF AT FIRST YOU DON'T SUCCEED

In a mythical land, in a mythical place, at a mythical time, there lived a King who ruled over a very interesting Kingdom, for it seemed that all of the subjects of this kingdom were the children of the King and there were many many of these subjects. Thousands, even. You might ask, "How is this possible?" But then, you would be forgetting that this is a mythical kingdom, and anything is possible in a mythical kingdom.

Although the people all had the same father, they did not all resemble each other in either face or form. In fact, some were quite beautiful, or handsome, as the case may be, while some were not; some were tall and some were short; some were thin and some were thick; some were highly intelligent, while some were not; some were rich and some were poor; some were healthy and some were sickly; and some were even born with handicaps. In between all these opposites types of people were the in between types. In other words, all the distributions seemed to be what one would expect in a society of so many people, and all the people accepted this as the normal state of affairs, and lived their lives accordingly.

But at this point in time, there was a great controversy raging amongst the people, for someone had found out that their mythical father in this mythical land, within this mythical place and time — the King — was not like any other King. It seemed that this King, their father, had the unusual ability to have each one of his children born into any one of these pairs of opposites that he desired. In other words, he could have one child born rich and handsome, and healthy and bright, while another might be born poor and plain, sickly and dull.

Well those that were born on the low end of these pairs of opposites were all in a buzz wondering why they were the ones that their father had chosen to suffer and not the other one. And, they wondered how come the father didn't choose everyone to be on the high end of the pairs of opposites, and even though there were also many middle types, it didn't seem quite fair to be looking up all the time.

When the king heard about all this buzzing, being the kind and loving and wise king that he was, he tried to make the people understand that even though he had the power to have any of his children born in any way that he wanted, that he didn't really have any choice in the matter, because his decisions were guided by a Higher Law. Everyone was who they were, living the life that they lived because of their own past actions. It was really out of his hands.

You can imagine what a can of worms this opened up. Some did not believe that the King had any power at all. Each household had the same question: "What does the King mean by telling us that our past actions are responsible for our suffering?" So, he replied to his people, because he wanted them to understand, "You have all lived before. Many times. And during those lives you created certain imbalances which you now need to balance out, and so, I placed each one of you into the position where you could best accomplish this."

Some would not accept this explanation, some did, some were not sure; some listened, some didn't. But, the King would answer no further questions. He would only say, "I love you all equally, for you are all my children and I have given each one of you the opportunity to grow and understand, and learn to work with the Higher Law until it is fulfilled. Each of you will find your own way in your own good time. Have faith and work towards that goal."

Chapter 15

Have you ever thought about this? If God is Love (as we are told) and we are all God's children (as we are told), then how is it that God does not appear to love us all equally (even though we are told that He does). Why do I say this? Well, just look around you. If we all live but one lifetime (as many believe), then why does it appear that God has not created us all equal?

Some people are born blind, some are born deaf, some are born crippled, some are born with disease-ridden bodies, some are born into extreme poverty, some are born into primitive and even cannibalistic societies; some are born with mental or physical limitations that make it impossible for them to function in society. Compare all these people to those who are born healthy, wealthy and wise. It is difficult to believe that we were all created equal. Of course, what we are observing is the manifest physical reality of the moment. If we were indeed all created equal in the physical realm when we were first "created," then why are all these differences so plainly visible? What we need to do is examine the phrase "created equal" from a spiritual perspective.

Continuing to look at the physical manifestation we can well ask whether this God loves all his children equally, or is God so whimsical and outright cruel to allow some of his children to suffer so miserably within their one lifetime. Is there only one opportunity for us to live before spending the rest of eternity in a Heaven or a Hell? Should we just shake our heads when confronted with this sadness and say, "It's God's Will" or perhaps, "Who can know the Will of God?" There is also the ever popular, "God moves in mysterious ways." Once again, we are compelled to ask: "How can God love His children equally?"

I said earlier in this book that I expected God to be reasonable, to make sense, and yet, what I have written in the above paragraphs would seem to indicate that this is not the case. But, as I have already said, "Things are not always what they appear to be."

But, I say that God is a God of Love, because God has created an ordered universe that is reasonable and makes sense. Our own actions result in very good reasons for apparent inequities in God's Love. And so, we must search for reasonable answers to the questions that have just been raised. And, as you may have guessed, the answers can be found within the concepts of Karma and Reincarnation! Karma and Reincarnation explains these apparent inequities, as well as several other questions not yet raised.

CHAPTER SIXTEEN
WHAT GOES AROUND, COMES AROUND

Buddhism: "By his divine vision a monk sees creatures who have fallen and have arisen, who are low and exalted, comely and ill-favored, fortunate and unfortunate, and he recognizes that creatures follow the destiny of their deeds."

Christianity: "Whatsoever a man soweth that shall he reap."

Confucianism: "Good and evil do not wrongly befall men, but Heaven sends down misery or happiness according to their conduct."

Hinduism: "As is an individual's desire, so is his will; and as is his will, so is his deed; and whatever deed he does, that will he reap."

Jainism: Every good will bear its fruit to men. Misery arises from wicked deeds. In this life and the next. People cannot escape the effects of their own actions."

Judaism: "Be sure, your sin will find you out."

Islam: "Every soul shall be recompensed for that which it has earned, and they shall not be wronged."

Sikhism: "As a man sows, so shall he reap: human life is lost without virtue."

Taoism: "The reward of good and evil follows as the shadow follows an object."

Zoroastrianism: "At the beginning of creation the Lord of Eternal Light established proper compensations for actions and words: a bad compensation for the bad — a good compensation for the good."

One could probably write several large books about the similarities of teachings to be found in the different scriptures of the world. Almost every one of these various religions feel that their Scripture is the true "Word of God." As Metaphysicists, or Esotericists, or philosophers, we hold that the "Truth" can be found in all the Scriptures, if one knows how to look for it. But, that is definitely the subject matter for another book. For now, let us just examine the excerpts from the various writings quoted above, for all of them describe the concept of Karma.

I purposely entitled this chapter as I have because this has become a popular expression of the day, and it is, in fact, a modern day description of Karma, though I would doubt that many people who use this expression recognize it as such.

As we study these excerpts, it is abundantly clear that you get back what you give out. In other words, whatever comes into your life is a result of your own previous actions. Edgar Cayce said, "You are constantly meeting (your)self," which is another way of saying the same thing.

Do you not see Karma's exquisite beauty, consistency with science, and the uncompromising justice of Creation, as a system which could only have been conceived within the Infinite "Mind of God?" Each and every one of the billions of lifestreams within this Cosmic scheme that lives on Planet Earth is receiving exactly what they have earned and deserve. That is the Law. That is the "Higher Law" of Karma.

Jesus said, Matthew 5.18: "For verily I say unto you, Till heaven and earth pass, one jot or one tittle shall in no wise pass from THE LAW (caps mine) till all be fulfilled." What are the "jots and the tittles"? A Jot is the smallest letter in the Hebrew alphabet; a Tittle is a mere ornamental curl of a Hebrew letter. What is THE LAW? It is the Law of Karma. In practical terms, these jots and tittles correspond to our every thought, feeling, word, and deed, i.e., they are the details of our daily lives. Again, Jesus, in Luke 16.17: And it is easier for heaven and earth to pass than one tittle of THE LAW to fail."

Chapter 16

We have seen, in some small measure, how this Law operates within the context of our discussion of thought-forms, how they permeate our aura, and, due to the electromagnetic quality of our aura, how the circumstances of our lives are drawn to us. That is how Karma manifests. What you give out is what you get back. Absolutely perfect! The difference between man-made laws and God's Laws? You may "get away" with breaking man's laws, but God's Laws? No way! The Law of Karma is in operation at all times, in all places, and you don't "get away' with any of those "jots and tittles."

But, what is the purpose of all this? Especially in light of the notion that much of your Karma is not due to activities in this life, but, has become manifest as a result of your activities in a previous life. Karma, therefore, implies Reincarnation — the idea that we have all lived many times before.

This is not a small concept. It deals with the reason we exist; purpose of life itself; and God's Plan for humanity. Reincarnation will therefore require further elaboration. But, before we tackle that issue, I would like to refer back to the last chapter, where I proposed to you that the apparent inequities of life, i.e., the differences between people and the circumstances of their lives are to be found in the Laws of Karma and Reincarnation.

> *In the mythical place and time of our mythical kingdom, our mythical King tried his best to respond to his people: "Why do we have to live multiple lives?" they asked, and "Why do we have to suffer and struggle so, when our King, our Father, has the power to just remove us from this situation and put us in a better place? Why can't we all go on to the next world — the Heavenly world — where it is peaceful, forgiving, and loving. Where it is a place of plenty for all, so that no man or woman will suffer?" And the people became restless and rebellious and demanded answers to their questions.*

The wise and loving King thought deeply and long before he answered, for he was afraid that the people would not understand. "My children," he said after much contemplation, "the Heaven world is not as you imagine it. Yes, it is a place of peace and love, but it is also a place of intense activity and even the smallest of negative thoughts would destroy the delicate fabric of the "higher" planes, this Heaven world." He paused, and in pausing, he was able to search the hearts and the minds of all his people. And, he saw that they could still not comprehend, so the King withdrew into his inner sanctuary to meditate for forty days and nights. He finally decided to send great Teachers to the people, who would live among them, and teach them all they needed to know. Several Great Ones, those who had already perfected the human experience, volunteered to return to the mythical kingdom and to be their Teacher.

Now, even though the King had meditated for forty days and nights, time seemed to "stand still" for the King as he meditated. Many, many years had passed for his people, and there was no longer anyone alive who had heard of the King's great power to have one of His children born into a given life situation. Once the King began to send teachers, they would teach people at the level they could understand.

The wise King chose a teacher who had demonstrated exceptional love and compassion in His earthly sojourns, and so, a Great One, came to teach the people of the Kingdom. When He reached the proper level of maturity, he began His Ministry, and He taught the people about Love; and He taught the people about the Law; the Universal Law. This He did in parables so that each who heard would be able to learn at their own level. Some learned at a superficial level, while some

Chapter 16

learned on a much deeper level. There were, of course, some who rejected both the Teacher, and his Teachings. The Great One addressed this problem: "He that hath ears to hear, let him hear, and he that hath eyes to see, let him see." and, "I speak to them in parables: because they, seeing, see not; and hearing, they hear not, neither do they understand."

Some understood the Law of Cause and Effect (Karma), because they had heard the teachings of the Great Teacher when he said: "Be ye perfect even as your Father in heaven is perfect." Therefore, they understood the purpose of existence, and the great goal that they must achieve. Unfortunately, there were many who did not understand, and some who thought, "He can't really mean "Perfect." How can I, a poor lowly human being, become perfect?" Of course, there were also those who didn't even bother to listen to the teaching.

But, that is exactly what He did mean. "Be ye Perfect even as your Father in Heaven is Perfect" is a command that all must follow. But, how do we become perfect? Well, do you remember how to sculpt an elephant? Get out the hammer and chisel and cut away everything that does not look like an elephant! Get out your hammer and chisel and start cutting away everything that is not perfect. We've talked about this before. We're talking about it again because it is the most important instruction that you will ever receive. This is your job. This is the reason for your being here on "Schoolroom Earth." In fact, everything that you think, feel, say or do, that is not directed toward this end, is a waste of time, and you will have to keep coming back to Schoolroom Earth until you succeed. Karma and Reincarnation are cause and effect. You will come back again and again and again, "until....," as my friend Tony Fisichella would say, "until you get it right!" Are we expected to become "Perfect" in one short lifetime? That would hardly seem practical, especially when we look around us, hard-pressed to find anyone who even approaches perfection, young or old. There are many blocks of marble with vaguely recognizable outlines, but very few well defined elephants taking shape. I guess that brings us around to reincarnation one more time...

CHAPTER SEVENTEEN
ONE MORE TIME......

Two gentlemen are having a conversation. One of them is complaining bitterly about his mother-in-law, who had to live in the same house with him: "Nag, nag, nag, complain, complain, complain. That woman is after me all the time, and I cant find any peace. And, she has this dog that yap, yap, yaps all the time. She's a dog of a woman herself, and I tell you, if she reincarnates as a dog then I want to reincarnate as the flea on her back!"

This so-called joke was told to me many years ago. I didn't think it was particularly funny then and my opinion of it hasn't changed with time. Why did I include it here? Because the circulation of such a "joke" is based on common misconceptions about the Law of Reincarnation.

A couple of years ago someone handed me a book to read that attempted to disprove Reincarnation. The book, written by a minister, was full of emotionally charged descriptions of reincarnation as a "horrendous" notion, and how unthinkable it was to imagine that a man could return as an animal. Confident that he had definitively proven his case, the author was sure that no one could refute his conclusions. Once again, however, this author expresses a distorted view of Reincarnation and why it exists.

We must be clear that Reincarnation exists for the purpose of evolution, not devolution. Let us understand that Reincarnation is not some "new age" doctrine followed by a few fringe groups. It is, in fact, a doctrine that is accepted by 2/3 of the world's population, and most of the world's major religions, with the exception of Christianity and Islam. Even Orthodox Judaism embraces Reincarnation. We should therefore not be too surprised to discover that the great teachers of early Christianity also taught it.

When I ask the students in my class, "How many of you believe in reincarnation?" a few hands go up. When I ask, "Who does not believe in reincarnation?" about an equal number of hands go up. Then I ask of those who have not responded, "Of those who have not yet raised their hands, how many accept the possibility of reincarnation?" and the rest of the hands go up. It is fair to say that this represents the majority. Then I ask them to list any objections to reincarnation, and based on these objections our discussion begins.

First, ask yourself if you are one of the ones who either believes in reincarnation or if you're open to the possibility of it. If you are a believer, you are in good company. Here is a small list of luminaries who believed in reincarnation: Socrates, Plato, Aristotle, Pythagoras, Leonardo Da Vinci, Spinoza, Voltaire, Benjamin Franklin, J. W. Von Goethe, William Wordsworth, Ralph Waldo Emerson, Henry David Thoreau, Walt Whitman, Edgar Allan Poe, Oliver Wendell Holmes, Richard Wagner, Leo Tolstoy, George Bernard Shaw, Arthur Conan Doyle, Henry Ford, Thomas Edison, Albert Einstein.[2] The list goes on and on, and although it is impressive, it proves nothing. So, let us turn to some of the questions and objections that have been raised in my class regarding this subject.

Objection #1: "If I have lived before, why don't I don't remember it?"

Before this question can be properly addressed, there are some basic things we need to know. First of all, you have not lived before. You are alive now and always have been — you are part of the Creator (Hylozoism). I am not suggesting that

---

[2] Joseph Head & S.L. Cranston, Reincarnation: the Phoenix Fire Mystery (New York: Julian Press/Crown Publishers)

Chapter 17

there is no such thing as reincarnation, but the personality that reincarnates is not you. You are your higher Self (or soul), which does reincarnate, and that part of you is eternal. The personality, or lower self, is temporary, and exists for only this incarnation. Incarnation means to be "in the flesh"— to re-incarnate means to be "in the flesh again." So, it is your soul which reincarnates. This body in which you now find yourself is brand new for this incarnation; it has a brand new brain, and that brain accumulates brand new memories for this life, but does not carry memories of your "past lives," which is really a blessing. You might wonder why I consider it a blessing?

Think about it. I don't know about you, but I've done some things in this life that I am not terribly proud of, and I'd be just as happy not to remember them. If the purpose of reincarnation is to evolve, it implies that in every incarnation prior to this one I was a less evolved being, and, being less evolved, I was prone to do things out of a less evolved consciousness. Since the more highly evolved ones consciousness becomes, the more loving and selfless one becomes, then it follows that a more lowly evolved consciousness would be less loving and more selfish. No doubt, I would have said and done things that I would probably find appalling, presuming that I now exist in a more evolved state. If I was a murderer, or a thief, or just a downright nasty individual in my earlier incarnations, I wouldn't want those memories floating around my consciousness today, so it is indeed a blessing that a "veil of forgetfulness" covers us from one incarnation to the next.

It is not the personality which reincarnates, but the soul, and the memories of each incarnation are embedded within your soul. When you gain soul consciousness, all of the memories of all of your lives will be like an open book to you that you can review at your leisure (After all, being eternal, you will have plenty of time). At that point, you would be able to view these memories with complete objectivity, from the perspective of an evolved being, and you will recognize all those experiences as having been necessary for your evolution toward the perfect being that God would have you be. Remember the saying of Jesus: "Be ye Perfect even as your father in heaven is Perfect."

Objection #2: "The idea that I might come back as an animal or an insect does not sit right with me."

As mentioned above, the idea of transmutation, that you may crossover to other species, and come back in some lower state of being. This is based on ignorance of the Law of Reincarnation, that derives from a larger "Law of Cycles." The Law of Cycles includes all cyclic activity, such as day following night, following day, etc., or the cyclic activity of the seasons, the tides, and so forth.

The purpose of reincarnation is the evolution of the soul. That evolution is an evolution of consciousness. Once again, we will state the basic principle of evolution — that consciousness does not go backward — it goes forward. Once having reached the state of consciousness of a human being, one does not go back to the consciousness of one of the lower animals, any more than an animal would go back to the consciousness of a plant or a rock.

This process of evolution is illustrated in the parable of the Prodigal Son who leaves his father's house and reaches the very depths of existence before turning his face back toward his father to begin his journey home. In a sense, we are all "Prodigal Sons," even those of us who have incarnated as females. The idea being, that we left "our Father's House" and incarnated into a material body in order to experience the material world. At some point the meaninglessness of physical plane existence comes to each of us, and we come to the realization that the pursuit of happiness in the material world is driven by desire and attachment, which ultimately leads us to unhappiness and despair. It is then that we will turn our face back to our Father's House (i.e., God, in Heaven) to begin our spiritual evolution. The earlier, material part of this journey consists of what we might call "involution." We may have started out as mere babes, but we return in all our maturity, having grown into an elevated state of consciousness to fulfill the promise of our journey as the Prodigal Son.

All of this does not happen in one lifetime. It takes many lifetimes to gain the experience and learn to grow in Wisdom and Understanding, and in our soul consciousness, so that we are fit to enter the "Kingdom of Heaven," which requires this "elevated state of consciousness" that we've been talking about.

Objection #3: (This is the big one for those of the Christian faith.) "If reincarnation is a fact, then why did Jesus not teach it?"

The response to this is a very interesting story which deserves a whole chapter of its own, and so we will resume this discussion in the next chapter.

CHAPTER EIGHTEEN
IT'S LIKE THIS...

In the sixth century AD there lived a lady named Theodora, a quite beautiful commoner, who caught the eye of the Emperor Justinian. He married her, and thus she became the Empress Theodora, who, along with her husband, had a devastating effect on history. Her friends were rewarded and her enemies were either imprisoned or mysteriously disappeared.
In "The Secret History," written not long after her death, Procopius of Caesarea writes that she was an actress and prostitute before becoming Empress.

She became horrified over the teachings of Origen, whom the Encyclopedia Britannica describes as "...the most prominent of the early Church fathers with the possible exception of St. Augustine" (who, by the way, taught reincarnation). Her horror resulted from Origen's teaching about reincarnation. From Origen's perspective she would probably not have been a beautiful Empress in a past life, and certainly would not be so in a future incarnation. This, no doubt, would have been intolerable to her, and she convinced Justinian to convene the Fifth General Ecumenical Council, which proceeded to declare all of Origen's teachings Anathema (cursed). As a result of this campaign, "The Three Chapters" in the Gospels referencing reincarnation were removed (as if saying it's not so will make it not so). The amazing thing is that this Ecumenical Council was not attended by the Pope, and it took years for its rulings to be recognized by the Church. Although the most significant references of reincarnation were removed, they did miss some passages that strongly imply reincarnation. From this point forward, Church doctrine would be resurrection and not reincarnation: "one life — then heaven or hell."

So there you have it...if you want it. To further complicate matters, when that Council was held, in 553 AD, Theodora had already died, but she had set it all up prior to her death, and Justinian followed through on her wishes.

If you think I made up this soap opera, let me assure you that though this is an abridged version of the facts, it has all been documented as church history.

And so, the truth of whether Jesus did, or did not, teach reincarnation has been obscured by the new direction Church doctrine took since the Fifth Ecumenical Council. On the other hand, since reincarnation was part of the Roman philosophy handed down from the Greeks (Pythagoras, Plato, et al.), and, since there is evidence to suggest that Jesus was raised by the Essenes (who definitely believed in reincarnation); and, considering that Orthodox Judaism has always believed in reincarnation; then it should not be too surprising to learn that the early Christian fathers, such as Saint Augustine, Saint Justin the Martyr, and Saint Gregory of Nyassa, taught reincarnation (and let's not forget Origen). It would be very strange if reincarnation was not part of Jesus' teachings. And, how about this ...

There is the story about the man who was born blind, and the disciples asked, "Who was it that sinned, the man or the parents, that the man had been born blind?" Jesus answered "Neither, but that the works (Laws) of God should be made manifest." If the man who was born blind was the sinner, then his sin could only have occurred in the material body of a former incarnation.

If you are really interested in Karma and Reincarnation, there are many fine books that deal with these subjects. One of the most interesting is "Esoteric Christianity," written by Annie Besant and published by Quest Books. Additionally, a book already mentioned, "Reincarnation: an east-west anthology," by Head and Cranston, was also published by Quest Books.

Now, what about the other side of the coin? What hard evidence, if any, do we have that Reincarnation exists? Probably none, but let us once again be reasonable. As I pointed out in our discussion of Karma, if this incarnation were the only one, it would be a very cruel and whimsical God that would make so many of His children suffer so. The only thing that makes any sense at all is that each and every individual currently incarnate (in a body) has been born into the absolutely perfect circumstances to allow for the growth of the soul on the path that leads to the fulfillment of Jesus's words: "Be ye Perfect, even as your father in heaven is Perfect."

I don't want to overstate this, but look around you and what you will see are people at different stages along this path toward perfection. Thieves, murderers, rapists, criminals of every kind are not as evolved as truly altruistic individuals such as Albert Schweitzer or Mother Theresa. These examples obviously describe extreme cases, but they illustrate the point. In between these extremes we see people that are more selfish and people that are less selfish; people that are more loving and giving, and people that are less loving and giving. This describes the various stages on the path to perfection.

What would a "Perfect" individual be like? They would be loving, kind, compassionate, selfless, helpful, wise, at all times, in all situations. All of the negative traits such as anger, greed, envy, selfishness and so on, would have been completely purged from their nature. Examine the life of Jesus, Buddha, and Krishna, etc., in light of all that's been said, and you will get the idea.

And what about the different talents and abilities that people are born with? How is it that Mozart could pick up a violin at age three and begin playing it without any instruction? How about child prodigies in the various fields of endeavor, including athletics? We must also wonder at the role that karma and reincarnation plays in the lives of "idiot savants," who are known for performing miraculous feats of memory, music and mathematics, though they are often unable to learn the simplest of academic lessons.

Without considering reincarnation, we are at a loss to provide

Chapter 18

a plausible explanation. However, when we consider karma and reincarnation, it all makes sense. The prima ballerina in this life danced in many choruses in previous incarnations. Their skills were learned through much hard work, over many lifetimes.

Then there are the people with memories of past lives, as well as many well-documented cases describing hypnotic regression through their past lives. There is also a book by Ian Stevenson that documents twenty cases of young children who remember their former lives in neighboring communities, naming people, places, and things that they could not possibly have any knowledge of. Hard proof? Not exactly, but very convincing anecdotal evidence within the context of everything we've been talking about.

Then there is the case of the rough and tumble fisherman, as reported in the Edgar Cayce readings. This individual, whose education did not go past the 6th grade, only knew how to fish. After a very severe accident he could no longer continue his work as a fisherman. He had a family to support, but he had no idea how he would do that. In a reading from Edgar Cayce, it was suggested that since he had been successful as an artist in a former incarnation, perhaps he should now pursue that as an occupation. Even though he had no inclination toward painting in this life, he gave it a try. It all came back to him very quickly, and in a short time he was selling his paintings and earning a very nice living.

Finally, if we refer back to Hylozoism, we realize that everything is alive, and being part of God, that life is eternal. It is not possible that we came into existence at birth. You can't create something new out of something which is already whole and complete. We exist "from everlasting to everlasting." In our soul nature we are eternal. So, fasten your seat belt, you're in for a very loooooong ride.

CHAPTER NINETEEN
NOW WHAT?

"Where ya goin'?"
"I dunno."
"Watcha gonna do when ya get there?"
"I dunno."
"If I was goin' somewhere, donchya think I'd know where I was goin?"
"I dunno."

We're all going somewhere. The problem is that most of us don't know it. Consider this: there's the mineral kingdom, the vegetable kingdom, the animal kingdom, the human kingdom and the Kingdom of Heaven, but we only call one of these kingdoms "a race." And, you're in the race (forgive the pun). The nice part about this race is that everybody (eventually) wins. The finish line — if you choose to call it that — is to enter the Kingdom of Heaven. So, what exactly is the Kingdom of Heaven?

It is the place that your soul dwells when you fulfill the words: "Be ye Perfect, even as your Father in Heaven is Perfect." When you reach this special place "you go no more out." In the New Testament's *Book of Revelation* 3:12: "Him that overcometh [the world] will I make a pillar in the temple of my God, and he shall go no more out" [reincarnate]. Heaven is where your soul lives when you have been Enlightened; Illuminated; Self-Realized; God-Realized, reached Nirvana, and so on.

It is, in fact, a place of elevated consciousness. So elevated, that once achieved, the individual finds that his consciousness no longer needs to reside in his lower vehicles. No longer does he think of himself as a personality, or identify himself with his physical, emotional and mental bodies. Instead, this entity <u>knows</u>

himself to be a spiritual being, with a consciousness that resides in his spiritual bodies, such as, the Atmic, Buddhic, and Manasic bodies that we spoke of earlier in this book. He <u>knows</u> himself consciously as a disembodied Soul, and eventually his consciousness resides in the Monad, at which point he <u>knows</u> himself to be "One with God" and "One with the Universe." I've underlined all the "knows" so as to distinguish them from "beliefs." You might recall our Chapter Two discussion about the difference between knowing and believing.

The Kingdom of Heaven, then, is not really a geographical place — it is a state of consciousness. An individual who has reached this state of consciousness might appear to us as all-wise, all-knowing, all-powerful, all-loving, and all-giving — almost superhuman. However, "the Kingdom" can only be gained through the hard work of purifying our lower vehicles, through selfless service, through study, and through meditation (sounds like another chapter to me).

How do we know that the Kingdom of Heaven exists? Because there have been those that have gone there before us and have returned to tell us about it, so we all may might learn what we need to do to gain the Kingdom, since that is the destiny of mankind. It is God's plan for us. It is God's will, and when God wills something, believe me, it will happen (eventually), but you have to earn the Kingdom yourself. The Way is there, the Path is accessible. There are those who will offer you a helping hand, but you're going to have to do it yourself. Who do we know that have gained the Kingdom? There is Jesus, Buddha, Krishna, Zarathustra, Lao Tzu, to name just a few.

Others that have successfully perfected themselves are known as Masters; Adepts; Ascended Beings; the Hierarchy; the Great White Brotherhood (so-called because of the brilliance of their aura). Incidentally, they are called "Masters," not because they are the master of anyone, but because they have mastered their lower natures. Some names that you may recognize are Kuthumi, El Morya, Djwhal Khul (the Tibetan) and Saint Germain. Don't worry if these names are unfamiliar to you. If you continue to pursue metaphysical studies, you will come across them.

Krishna, Buddha, and Jesus taught the Law in their own way in their own time. The underlying theme of all of the scriptures of the world teach the same Law. The Masters taught the Law in ancient times through what has become known as "Mystery Schools." In modern times they have brought the Law to man through their disciples who have transcribed and interpreted the Laws for mankind. Of these more modern teachings, among the most significant was given to us through H.P. Blavatsky in 1875 within two volumes known as "The Secret Doctrine," published by The Theosophical Society. The "Secret Doctrine" was the first of these ancient teachings to be presented to modern man and especially to the Western world. It is very difficult to understand, but it was a tremendous breakthrough, and it is still extremely valuable for those who are able to study and comprehend it. The Masters Kuthumi and El Morya were instrumental in bringing it forth.

Starting in the 1920's, the Master Djwhal Khul is said to have brought forth eighteen volumes (published by the Lucis Trust), through his disciple, Alice A. Bailey. These volumes were an elaboration and expansion upon Blavatsky's "Secret Doctrine." Like the Secret Doctrine, these books are difficult to understand, but they comprise an outstanding body of work describing what has been called "The Ageless Wisdom."

In addition to the written work that the Masters have brought forth, they work with individual *chelas* (students/disciples) guiding them into service activities that will be beneficial to mankind. They also do whatever they can to influence world leaders to bring peace, understanding and harmony to the world. They do, however have their own "prime directive" and may not directly interfere. As painful as our "growing pains" may be, we must all learn to "do it ourselves."

Chapter 19

Those Great Beings that have gained their ascension could have moved on to other realms of the Kingdom but have chosen to remain here to help redeem all of humanity so that each and every individual can achieve their "ascension" and gain the "Kingdom of Heaven," at which time there will be a true Paradise on earth.

If you are interested in finding out more about the Masters I recommend reading "The Golden Thread" by Natalie Banks, published by Lucis Trust, as well as "The Masters and the Path" by C. W. Leadbeater, published by The Theosophical Publishing House.

So you see the purpose of all these incarnations and reincarnations is to learn how not to keep doing it. I quoted my good friend Tony earlier, when someone asked him how many times do we have to keep coming back....?

"UNTIL YOU GET IT RIGHT!"

Did you get that? Well, what are you waiting for? Get to work!

CHAPTER TWENTY
NOW YOU'VE GOT IT ... YOU THINK

> A little fun with Descartes:
> "I think, therefore I am."
> I think, therefore I am - I think
> I think I think, therefore I am thinking
> I think I think, therefore I am thinking I am
> I think I am thinking, therefore I am thinking I am
> I think I am thinking I am, therefore I am thinking I am
> I think I am thinking, therefore, I am thinking I am thinking I am
> I think I am thinking I am, but if I'm not, I may not be and therefore, am I?

Now you think you've got it, and if you do, now that you've got it, what are you going to do with it? Have you really got it? Do you?

Well, if you've really got it, then you know what to do. You know that you are involved in an evolutionary process that is leading you toward perfection. You know how to chip away at the imperfections until all that is left is perfection. You know about the As-if technique, the Visualization technique, and the process of Precipitation. You know how to be the Observer. You know that you are the Prodigal Son on his return journey home.

What you may not know is that all of these things are part of walking "The Path," for the Path is the road to perfection, and you have been on the Path all along if you've followed the instructions given to you until this point in the book. You are already on your way to the Kingdom. You are on your way to fulfilling your destiny and completing your part of God's Plan. You are on your way to becoming an Ascended Master. Yes, you. You can do it too. Remember, you and I are part of God and we have infinite potential.

All you have to do is become more loving, more giving, more

caring, more understanding, more patient, more tolerant, more compassionate, more helpful, more selfless, more harmless (in the sense that you would never harm anyone or anything), and you have to learn to "love your neighbor as yourself" — if for no other reason than your neighbor is yourself — and we're all part of the One.

The choice is yours. You can go back to living your life in the same manner as you always have (been there, done that), or, you can now make a conscious effort to move forward along the Path.

Maybe the following will help you along the way: We have been told by those who know and have been there themselves, that there are three things that we must do in order to gain the Kingdom of Heaven:

Study, Meditate, Serve

Study: Study the books that are going to give you a good foundation in Metaphysics and Spirituality, and stay away from those that are dealing with phenomena; psychism, channeling, and the like. At the end of the book, in Appendix A, I will give you a bibliography of books that should give you a good foundation so you will have a solid base against which to measure new material that passes your way.

Meditate: Meditation teaches you to still your lower bodies and to make contact with your Higher Self. Meditation is the subject of the next chapter.

Service: Service is considered the main tool for making progress along the Path. It balances out the Karma that you have accumulated from lifetime to lifetime. Service is sometimes defined as "Seeing a need and filling it." In order for service to be effective it has to be done selflessly, that is, with no thought for oneself,

Many who begin to walk the Path, once having recognized the

importance of service, are at a loss to understand what that service should be. It does not have to be earth shattering. Not everyone is going to be a Mother Theresa or an Albert Schweitzer. Service can be a friendly "Hello," a word of encouragement, a pat on the back, or a helping hand whenever and wherever it is needed.

Begin serving wherever you find yourself. Within your own family, at work, around your community. It has been said that "The reward of service is the opportunity for greater service," and that's true. Just begin by being selfless in your service and you will be amazed at the opportunities that open up to you. Just make sure that the service is selfless with no thought for reward of any kind. For example: You hold the door open for someone behind you and the person just walks by you, ignoring you completely. What's your response? Are you annoyed and do you say to yourself sarcastically "Well, thank you!" If that is your response then you have to ask yourself why you held the door open in the first place. Was it to be of service, or was it because you were looking for that "Thank you." Be the Observer. View yourself objectively and examine your motive. That's what counts. Keep your motives pure and you will have no problem with service.

Now on to meditation.

CHAPTER TWENTY-ONE
THINK ABOUT IT

> Until one is committed
> there is hesitancy, the chance to draw back,
> always ineffectiveness.
> Concerning acts of initiative (and creation)
> there is one elementary truth
> the ignorance of which kills countless ideas
> and splendid plans:
> That the moment one definitely commits oneself
> then Providence moves too.
> All sorts of things occur to help one
> that would never otherwise have occurred.
> A whole stream of events issues from the decision,
> raising in one's favor all manner
> of unforeseen incidents and meetings
> and material assistance
> which no man could have dreamt
> would come his way.
> Whatever you can do, or dream you can, begin it.
> Boldness has genius, power, and magic in it.
> Begin it now.   -Goethe

There is nothing terribly difficult or mysterious about meditation. You already know how to meditate, although you might not realize it!

You think not? Has there ever been a time when you made plans in your mind about anything, be it a vacation, a job interview, or how you are going to go about doing something, or any one of a thousand things where you had to mentally envision yourself in a given situation? Have you ever spent time going over and over in your mind something that was worrying you or bothering you; perhaps there was some important decision that you had to make? If you have, then you've been meditating. You may not consider this to be meditation because you think there needs to be something mysterious and mystical about it, but it is a form of meditation, just the same. Now, all we need to do is transform this meditation from the mundane into the spiritual.

Just a note of caution here: If you are meditating (thinking or worrying) about negative things, that is what you will draw into your life. (Please review Chapter Twelve on thought-forms and precipitation.)

The word meditation is derived from the Latin prefix *medi*, which means middle. So, meditation is a middle principle, one that bridges the gap from one state of consciousness to another. No matter what level you reach, meditation is the tool that will help you to achieve the next level, and being part of an Infinite Being, there is no end to these levels.

In meditation, the object is to still the lower bodies (physical, emotional and lower mental) so that contact can be made with your Higher Self. Remember, half the mental body is part of your personality, while the "other half" partakes of your Spirituality. This is the point where your lower self and higher Self are in the closest proximity, and it is where communication can take place between them.

Once you have quieted the lower bodies, you need to then focus on some words (sometimes called a seed thought), or object, that are of a higher vibration. This will raise the vibration of your lower self until it is closer in nature to the Higher.

When you first begin to do a spiritual meditation, your lower bodies are going to resist. They like the rate of vibration just the way it is. After all, they created it, they are in control, and now here you are trying to upset things, trying to switch to some new vibration, insisting that they do what you want them to do. Well, that's the point of the entire exercise. Your personality has been in control for far too long. Now it's time for the "Real You" to take over!

So, the first thing that will happen to most people when they

Chapter 21

try to still the lower bodies, is that the lower bodies rebel. All of a sudden you find that you are itching in places that you didn't even know existed. Emotional things will pop up to distract you, and your mind will start wandering all over the place. Don't get discouraged. Persevere. Eventually, your lower bodies will see that you mean business, and will come into line with what your Higher Self desires. You will no longer be a puppet on a string, being pulled this way and that at the whimsy of your lower bodies. Eventually, they will become calm, peaceful and quiescent, no longer a concern, and they will fade into the background, empowering your Real Self to take over. Now, we can begin the true work of meditation. Here are some hints that may help you with your meditation:

1. Find a quiet place where you can be free from interruptions or sensory distractions.
2. Seat yourself comfortably with back erect, but not stiff, head level, eyes closed and hands folded in your lap or palms facing up. You have to be as relaxed as possible.
3. Meditate daily. Meditation requires practice.
4. Try to meditate in the morning. The thought atmosphere is clearer at that time.
5. If possible, meditate in the same spot at the same time every day. This area will build up a good vibrational field that will make it easier for you to get into meditation, and lift you to a higher level. If that is not possible on any particular day, then meditate wherever and whenever you can. Don't skip days if you can help it.
6. Know that the purpose of meditation is to contact your Higher Self and listen for what has been called "the still, small voice within."
7. Begin your meditation by relaxing and quieting your lower bodies. If your mind wanders, don't get upset, just gently guide it back to the purpose at hand.
8. Some like to begin their meditation with a prayer, such as the

Lord's Prayer.
9. Go into your meditation with a "seed thought" as described earlier. (I will give you a number of possibilities in the Appendix.) When working with a seed thought, examine it from all sides. You may feel that you are just thinking about it, but you will find that you gain some insights from it that you would not get just from thinking. Your Higher Self will subtly feed you this information which will prove valuable to your spiritual growth.
10. Meditate for short periods of time at first, gradually increasing to at least a half hour per day.
11. Possible steps, then, would be: Relax; Pray; Concentrate; meditate on a seed thought; Send out blessings to the world, or close with another prayer or the Great Invocation (See Appendix).

It has been said that there are as many forms of meditation as there are people meditating. You will find that which is most comfortable and beneficial for you. The main thing is to begin today. Meditation might be considered just another spiritual tool, but, it is really the key to our spiritual progress. But, you must put it into action for it to be of any benefit to you.

The opening quote to this chapter from Goethe applies to all aspects of the spiritual path. Begin today. Do it now. Tomorrow becomes yesterday soon enough.

CHAPTER TWENTY TWO
THINK ON THESE THINGS

Buddha taught the Four Noble Truths:
1. Existence is unhappiness.
2. Unhappiness is caused by selfish craving (attachment).
3. Selfish craving (attachment) can be destroyed.
4. It can be destroyed by following the Noble Eight-Fold Path:
    1. Right knowledge (understanding)
    2. Right thought
    3. Right speech
    4. Right activity (conduct)
    5. Right vocation (occupation)
    6. Right effort
    7. Right memory (mindfulness)
    8. Right concentration (meditation)

A seed-thought may be a word, a phrase, a line from a poem, a quote from scripture, or any uplifting idea that will tend to raise your vibratory rate. Here are a number of ideas that I have gathered together that may be useful to you:

- Harmlessness (to not be harmful)
- Not my will, but Thine, Oh Lord, be done in me and through me
 May I ever be a channel of blessings to all that I contact in every way.
 Let my going in and my coming out be in accord with that Thou would have me do
 And as the call comes, here am I, send me, use me
 - Edgar Cayce
- Having pervaded the world with a fraction of my self; I yet remain - Bhagavad-Gita

- From the unreal lead me to the Real
- From darkness lead me to light
- From death lead me to immortality
- The Lord's Prayer (or any part it)
- Love is the fulfilling of the Law - St. Paul
- Blessed are they which do hunger and thirst after righteousness: for they shall be filled
  - Jesus: The Sermon on the Mount
- Mind is the source of happiness and unhappiness - Buddha
- Let your light so shine before men, that they may see your good works, and glorify your Father which is in heaven - Jesus
- What a man wants is already within him -Sri Ramakrishna
- When the heart weeps for what it has lost, the spirit laughs for what it has found -Sufi aphorism
- The One God hidden in all living beings
- The Living Witness biding in all hearts
- The wise who seek and find Him in the Self. To them, and none else, is eternal joy -The Vedas
- Love is my golden touch
  It turns desire into service - from a Baul song
- Love itself is the original substance of love; Reverence is love in graceful expression; Righteousness is love in judgment; and Wisdom is love in discriminating -Chu Hsi
- A truly virtuous man cannot be injured. One who attempts an attack upon him is like a man who flings dust at another while the wind is contrary - Buddha
- Know Thyself
- To see the world in a grain of sand
  And Heaven in a wild flower
  Hold infinity in the palm of your hand
  And eternity in an hour -William Blake
- Who am I? What is the nature of that part of me which is not subject to change? What is my purpose in life?

- 0 Thou, Who givest sustenance to the Universe
  From Whom all things proceed,
  To Whom all things return,
  Unveil to us the face of the true Spiritual Sun
  Hidden by the disc of golden light
  That we may know the Truth
  And do our whole duty
  As we journey to thy sacred feet.
- Lord, make me an instrument of your peace
  Where there is hatred, let me sow love
  Where there is injury, pardon
  Where there is doubt, faith
  Where there is despair, hope
  Where there is darkness, light
  And where there is sadness, joy
  0 Divine Master, grant that I may not so much seek to be consoled, as to console
  To be understood, as to understand
  To be loved as to love
  For it is in giving that we receive
  It is in pardoning that we are pardoned
  And it is in dying that we are born to eternal life
  - Prayer of Saint Francis

Any of the above seed thoughts will aid you to attain higher levels of consciousness. You may use the same ones over and over and continue to gain insights from them. You will no doubt come across others in your reading and studying. Use them. They will help you along the Path. They will help you to reach what is for now, your ultimate goal.

CHAPTER TWENTY-THREE
YOU ASKED FOR IT

Ask, and it shall be given you; seek and ye shall find; knock, and it shall be opened unto you - Matthew

Therefore, I say unto you, what things soever ye desire, when ye pray, believe that ye receive them, and ye shall have them - Mark 11.24

There was this very devout man who spent many hours of each day praying. Sometimes he prayed for others, but most of the time he prayed for himself. Sometimes his prayers were answered, but most times, not. In the fullness of time this man passed on to the next realm and when he was met by Saint Peter at the gate he couldn't wait to ask why so many of his prayers were not answered. Saint Peter said, "Wait here and I'll go and find out." After a time Peter came back. "The Boss says your prayers were always answered, but most of the time the answer was No!"

There are many ways that we can approach God. I would like to discuss two of these which have the greatest immediacy and practicality at the present time. Prayer, which is an asking of God; and Affirmation, where you affirm something about yourself, or yourself in relation to God.

One way is not better than any other, for both are putting energy out into the Universe, energy that will always elicit a like response. However, there are effective ways and ineffective ways to approach these methods. First, we'll examine prayer, by asking: What's wrong with this picture?

Chapter 23

"Oh, God, just let this shot go in." (Prayed to a ball shot at the final buzzer of a basketball game by the team one point behind.) "Oh, God, please don't let this shot go in." (Prayed by the opposing team.)

What's wrong with this picture?

"Oh, God, just let the ball go in the hole." (Prayed for any game where balls go in holes.)

"Oh, God, make it miss." (Prayed by anyone who stands to lose if this particular ball goes in this particular hole.)

Remember, while you are praying for your team to win, the other team is praying for their team to win. The team that wins says, "My prayer has been answered." The team that loses thinks, "God didn't answer my prayer." You can't have it both ways. As a result, there is much confusion concerning prayers. On the one hand, we are told that prayers are always answered. On the other hand, we may observe that this does not seem to be the case in most instances. People pray for a lot of things that they don't get. Is the little story about the answer sometimes being "No," true? I think not, though it may at times seem that way.

If the story were true, then that would seem to imply a God that has a personality like you and me, who fields all these requests (prayers), and then arbitrarily makes decisions. This one, "yes"; this one "no"; this one "maybe"; this one, "not now, but hang in there, maybe later," and so on. The idea of God sitting on His "Throne of Glory" somewhere in Heaven creates God in man's image rather than the other way around.

Let us take a look at the larger picture. The Universe is where we exist, live and move. Every thought, every feeling, every word, every action has its effect upon the Universe. Let us liken that effect to a ripple in a pond after we drop a pebble into it. The ripple goes out to the shore and then returns from whence it came. The Universe acts as a perfect reflector. What you send out is what you get back. In that respect, every prayer is "answered." The prayer is sent out into the Universe, which can really do nothing but reflect that prayer back to its sender. That is the nature of the Universe. It is not arbitrary. It is governed by Law, which is both natural and divine. Please review Chapter Twelve on thought-forms and Chapter Sixteen on Karma, if we need to refresh our memory on how this all works.

Why is it, then, that so many prayers seem to be unanswered? Let me repeat the quote from Saint Mark given above: "Therefore, I say unto you, what things soever ye desire, when ye pray. Believe that ye receive them, and ye shall have them." (Mark 11.24). If you are praying to win the lottery, but in the back of your mind you really believe you won't win it, then your prayer is being "answered" just as you sent it out — filled with negativity. What you really believe is that you won't win the lottery, and that is what the Universe hears, and so the prayer is "answered" appropriately: "Okay, you won't win the lottery." You see, it's not the words themselves, but the thought behind the words that the Universe is responding to. You can't fool yourself, so don't think that you can fool the Universe (God). "Be not deceived; God is not mocked — for whatsoever a man soweth, that shall he also reap." (Galatians 6.7)

Earlier I suggested that there are effective ways of praying and ineffective ways of praying. Prayers which are directed toward self (little self, that is) will be ineffective. Selfish prayers, like selfish thought-forms are just going to hang around your aura.

Prayers such as "God, if you'll only do this for me, (whatever: a new car; get me out of trouble; let me win this once, etc. Then I'll be good from now on). This will not get the job done. As Edgar Cayce put it; "God is not your messenger boy." In order to make this perfectly clear, we need to ask and answer a couple of questions:

1. What exactly do we mean when we say that a prayer has been answered?
2. Is it true that every prayer receives an answer?

To answer question #1, people consider that their prayer has been answered if they pray for something and it appears in their life just as they prayed for it. For example: A man is walking down the street and he prays to God; "God, let me find a $100 dollar bill lying on the street as I turn this next corner," and lo and behold, he turns the corner and there, lying in the street is a $100 dollar bill being held down by a brick so that it won't blow away. "Ah," cries the man, "my prayer has been answered."

Same scenario. A man walking down the street prays to God; "God, let me find a $100 dollar bill lying in the street as I turn this next corner," and lo and behold, he turns the corner and there is no brick, and no $100 dollar bill. The man says, "My prayer has not been answered." But, I would suggest that the second man's prayer was answered just as clearly as the first man's prayer. What was the difference? The first man had total faith in God to provide what was needed, and this money was needed to save another man's life. (Okay — a little dramatic, but you get the point.) The second man never believed, or had real faith that there would be money lying in the street. And, he would only spend it frivolously anyway. The thought and intention behind his prayer was that it will never be answered, and so, it appeared to go unanswered.

To answer question# 2, every prayer does receive an answer. Prayer is a form of energy put out into the Universe and the Universe must respond in a like manner (remember, that's the Law). The Universe responds in direct proportion to the amount of energy that is sent out. Prayers are generally said fervently and contain a great deal of energy. When a prayer seem to be unanswered, it is because we either do not see, do not hear, do not recognize, or do not understand the answer. Prayers need to be said in an effective way in order for them to receive the response that we are seeking. As indicated above, praying selfishly is an ineffective way to pray. Can we define effective prayer?

1. The prayer needs to be selfless and directed for the benefit of others. If the prayer is about yourself, then it should be a selfless request to become a greater instrument of service, and a channel of blessings to all that you contact in every way.

2. The prayer has to be sincere with the thought behind the prayer matching the words that are being spoken.
3. The prayer should be said with a great intensity of feeling behind it.
4. Repetition of the prayer is helpful.
5. Visualize the prayer as being answered the instant that it is given. Again I refer you to Mark 11.24, as quoted above. You have to believe with all your heart that the prayer is answered. Have faith. You are a child of God and God will not forsake His children. (The guy who found the $100 dollar bill obviously had that faith.)

It is important to note that even prayers delivered effectively, with faith and fervor, may sometimes be answered in a way that we either do not understand, or in a way that we did not expect. But, that may be because we don't always know what is right for ourselves or for other individuals. The Higher Self has its own agenda, and that agenda will always take priority. The following prayer, written by Simons Roof, is an example of a prayer which asks that you may be a greater instrument of service for the benefit of others:

Give us the will
which knowing human need
makes us cooperators
with the Divine Plan

Give us the love
which making all men one
turns our star of suffering
into a world of peace.

Give us the wisdom
which responding to the Master (Jesus)
makes us channels
of His spirit on earth.
Give us will and love and wisdom

which knowing human need
which making all men one
which responding to the Master
Makes each one of us
a source of His light
a center of His love
and brothers in His life.
Amen

    Now read the prayer of Saint Francis again, in light of what we have been talking about:

Lord, make me an instrument of your peace
Where there is hatred, let me sow love
Where there is injury, pardon
Where there is doubt, faith
Where there is despair, hope
Where there is darkness, light
and where there is sadness, joy
0 Divine Master, grant that I may not so much seek to be consoled, as to console
To be understood, as to understand
To be loved as to love
For it is in giving that we receive
It is in pardoning that we are pardoned
And it is in dying that we are born to eternal life

    That is why Jesus knew that he must teach his disciples the correct way to pray. These marvelous prayers, such as the Lord's Prayer, and the 23rd Psalm, are wonderful to meditate upon, either in part, or the complete prayer.
    I would like to share another beautiful prayer with you which also contains much material for meditation.

Oh thou infinite Holy Presence of God, the Divine Source of all life,
Hallowed be Thy Sacred Name!
We bow before Thee in gratitude, praise and thanksgiving
For Thy Supreme Presence in the Universe...
Because Thou Art... I AM!
We return to Thee, Almighty One, all the Power and Dominion
We have ever vested in any imperfect manifestation, visible or invisible, for Thou Art the All-Power of the Universe, and there is no other Power that can act!
Let Thy Will be done in us now!
Let Thy Kingdom be manifest across the face of the Earth
Through the hearts of all who are so blessed as to live upon it.

Oh Supreme beloved One, as we lift our hearts,
Our vision, our consciousness toward Thee,
Release the substance of Thyself to us, each according to our requirements,
That as we move forward in Thy Name, and upon Thy Service,
We shall not be found wanting.

We ask forgiveness for all the transgression of Thy Law of Love and Harmony,
Both for ourselves and all mankind,
The forces of the elemental Kingdom and the Kingdom of nature.
Endow us with Thy Power and Desire
To so forgive all who have ever caused us distress
Back into the very beginning of time.

Because Thou Art with us and in us, we fear no evil,
For there is no power apart from Thee
Which can hurt, destroy or despoil Life's beauty of expression.
Thou art the strength and the power
By which we move ever in the Path of Righteousness,
And now, Oh Father of Light, show us the Full glory

We had with Thee in the beginning before even this world was! This we ask IN THY MOST HOLY NAME... I AM!"

It is good to pray for others as long as you don't impose your own will (it is not for you to say what another's soul purpose or Karma is) and if you qualify your prayer with "Let Thy Will be done, Father," you may pray that another be filled with Light and Love and be uplifted that they might find their own way. You may pray for peace and harmony between yourself and another or between other individuals, or for all the nations of the world. And remember, you may pray for yourself as long as your motive is to be used as an instrument for God's purposes. What you want to do is be a channel through which blessings flow to others. In the next chapter, we will cover Affirmations.

CHAPTER TWENTY-FOUR
WHAT DO YOU SAY?

What you think, you become (Precipitation). What you say adds power to what you think (Affirmation). Think before you speak. Think about what you think and what you say will take care of itself! When God created the Universe, He thought about it first, and then He spoke the Word. You are created in God's image. You create in the same manner as God. I've pointed this out to you in Chapter Twelve when we discussed Thought-forms. (Please review Chapter Twelve. It is important that you have a clear understanding of Thought-forms and Precipitation to gain the full value of what Affirmations can bring into your life).

Does any of this sound all too familiar to you? "I'm no good at that." I'm just too tired.""I'm so clumsy, I even trip over the flowers in the carpet." "I'm not smart enough." "I'm not clever enough." "I'm too dumb to do that." "I never win at anything." "I'll never get that job." "I'll never have enough money." "I'm not worthy." "I'm just not good enough." "That's the way I am, that's the way I'll always be and nothing can change that."

Heard enough? Should I stop there? Are these statements of fact, or are they self-fulfilling prophecies? I'll tell you what they are — they are all Affirmations. Unfortunately, they are all negative Affirmations. We affirm things about ourselves all the time. We affirm things about ourselves all the time, and we do so without thinking. The old adage "Think before you speak" holds true. The spoken word is so powerful that you can change your life by what you say about yourself. That is what Affirmation is all about.

Here is another situation where we don't have to learn how to Affirm, we have to learn what to Affirm. Do you sometimes Affirm good things about yourself? Good. Whatever you Affirm about yourself will eventually manifest in your life. Affirmations are like super-charged Thought-forms. They attract like vibrations to themselves and eventually Precipitate into your life.

But Affirmations go further. When you repeat an Affirmation you attract those vibrations into your Aura. You are affirming what it is that you would like to see in your life, and if you stick with it, and affirm with intensity, truly believing and knowing that what you are affirming will appear in your life ... it will!

Just a few more things to mention before I provide you with some examples of Affirmations. Affirmations that begin with I AM are the most powerful because I AM are words of Power. It is important to remember that if you say an Affirmation, but in the back of your mind you are saying "Oh yea, fat chance of that ever happening," then you are negating the Affirmation. For example, if you Affirm, "I Am a winner. All good things in life will come to me," but, in the back of your mind you are saying, "Fat chance, etc.," Forget about it! It's never going to happen!

Most of the time you will be affirming something that is not true in your life at the moment. But, that's the whole point of an Affirmation! The Affirmation is designed to make those things manifest in your life. You are sending out the vibrations of what you want to become, and these vibrations attract those things into your life since like attracts like. (See, I told you that you need to review Chapter Twelve).

But, just as with Prayer, your Affirmations need to be selfless, not selfish. An Affirmation such as: "I Am a rich guy. I want lots of money so that I can buy lots of things for myself," that's not exactly what we have in mind here.

One more thing, never affirm negatively. You will still be drawing the vibrations of that negativity into your life. "I will not be angry. I will not be angry! I WILL NOT BE ANGRY!" is still focusing on the vibrations of anger. Rather, say, "I AM calm, loving and peaceful at all times and in all situations." So always be careful how you word the Affirmation. The Universe will respond to exactly what you are Affirming.

Following, are a few Affirmations that you might use. Modify them to suit your needs. Use what feels right to you. Make up your own to fit your situation.

- I AM the Master of my life.
- I AM the only governing presence in my life.
- I AM a totally loving being.
- I AM a being of Love and Light
- I AM creating perfect peace and harmony in my life (or between us)
- Day by day, and in every way, I AM becoming more relaxed, peaceful and more loving.
- I AM a winner. All good things in life are drawn to me.
- Because I AM a force for good, I magnetically attract to me all the good in the Universe.
- I AM a Divine Magnet, attracting all positive things into my life.
- I AM One with the Power that created me.
(When having a disagreement, say...) *Namaskara* which means, "I salute the Divinity in you."
- I AM now creating my life the way I want it to be.
- I AM a channel for the Creative Power of the Universe.
- I AM living in harmony with the Universe.
- I AM a channel of blessings to all that I contact.
- I AM loving, kind, patient and understanding at all times, both to myself and others.
- I AM attracting health, joy and abundance into my life.
- I AM creating positive results on all levels of my life.
- I AM achieving all of my goals easily.
- I AM a Divine Being that never fails or makes a mistake.
- I AM Perfection manifesting in every cell of my being.
- I AM always demonstrating perfect poise, controlling all situations harmoniously through Divine Love.
- I AM relaxed, calm and peaceful at all times, in all situations.
- I AM re-creating every cell of my body in perfect health.

Chapter 24

As pointed out earlier, "I AM" are words of power and so all of the above Affirmations begin with "I AM." However, just saying "I" (the first part of I AM), also has power and is effective in drawing those vibrations into your aura. For example: "I always do and say the right thing at the right time in the right place."

Here is a wonderful, but somewhat lengthy, affirmation. It comes from the book "Melchizedek Truth Principles" by Frater Achad:

I am now in the presence of Pure Being.
I behold no other radiance than the radiance of the Christ Light
Of which I am a divine part.
I am now fully conscious of the presence of the indwelling God.
I now behold the Living Christ of God, in whose image and likeness
I AM.
I ascend in consciousness and stand before the altar
Which I have created through my desire of oneness
With the Infinite Supreme Principle of the Universe.
That Principle which has brought all life into manifestation.
I am no longer part of doubt or fear.
I am at peace with all mankind through the Love of the Living God.
I behold nothing but perfection,
I see all mankind in perfect spiritual accord.
I proclaim peace on earth, as it is in Heaven.
Nothing can separate me from the Living God.
I send forth thoughts of Love to all those who may be
In understanding less fortunate than myself.
I bathe them, spirit, soul and body, and see them continually bathed
With the goodness and Greatness of God's Love.
There is no confusion in the Universe. I see none, I hear none.
I hear but the voice of God and I feel the Presence of God's
Oneness throughout the Universe.
I see youth in all that which expresses Life, I see Life eternal.
I do not, I cannot behold or become a part, for myself or my fellow man,

Of that which man has learned to call death;
I see Health, Peace, Life in every full measure of abundance
Wherever Life is expressed;
I am One with the Living God; I see no defeat.
I do not know or understand what man has called annihilation.
Every good purpose and every good deed;
Every good act, every good thought, continues its growth
Throughout the Universe.
I am now in the Presence of Pure Being.
And all of that which I shall ever become a part of;
Rests in the Presence of Pure Being.
I know no malice, no contempt,
I am one with God and my fellow man
So make it be.

Amen

Chapter 24

CHAPTER 25
READ ANY GOOD BOOKS LATELY?

I used to read a lot of Science Fiction. Back in the early days there was a character named "Lefty Feep." Lefty was connected with a mad professor who had invented a time machine and was always sending Lefty somewhere in time for one adventure after another. In this particular episode, there was a giant computer that had taken over the world (this was years ago before computers had actually taken over the world), and Lefty had to figure out a way to stop the computer before all the inefficient people were eliminated. Lefty's solution was to devise a problem that the computer couldn't solve, and the computer would blow itself up trying to figure it out. This is what Lefty did, and as planned, the computer blew itself up and Lefty saved the world. The problem that Lefty posed was in the form of a question, "What's the difference between a duck?"

When Lefty returned from his time travels to the present (his present), he related his experience to the professor and the professor marveled over Lefty Feep's ingenuity, "Of course there is no answer to the problem," said the professor. "But, of course, there is," replied Lefty. The solution to the problem is this: "It has one leg both the same!"

The solution kind of sounds like a Zen meditation *kōan*, similar to, "What is the sound of one hand clapping?"

What's the point of relating this story here? There is none. And, if you are going to try to make sense out of the question, and answer, then your brain will probably explode just like the computer's. It's just that I found this story amusing fifty years

Chapter 25

ago, and it has stuck with me ever since, so I thought I would share it with you since this chapter is about books, good and otherwise.

Thirty years or so ago, if you became interested in Metaphysics, you would be hard-pressed to find any books on the subject at your local bookstore. You had to visit a bookstore that specialized in books of that nature. In today's world, every bookstore contains several sections dealing with Metaphysics and related subjects under headings such as: "New Age," "Metaphysics," "Philosophy," "Religion," and even "Bible Study" sections.

The problem today is not having enough books but having too many books. The market has become flooded with books as interest in the subject has grown. The reason I say that there are too many books, is that, unfortunately, not all of those books are of equal value. Some are of little value and some can be misleading and downright harmful to the beginner. Many deal with psychic phenomena which will tend to lead you down a side path rather than on "The Path" that I spoke about earlier. And, after all, I don't want your brain to explode.

I believe that the proper course is to read and study some books that are "tried and true." Learn from these studies. Learn from your meditations. Learn from your experiences as you use the tools that I have given you in this book. And, in so doing, you will be building a solid frame of reference from which you can evaluate some of the many books that are out there. Some of them are quite valuable, but you have to grow in what we in Esoteric studies call "Discrimination" and "Discernment." To that end, I have selected a number of books that I feel good about. I will list them in their order of difficulty and try to give you a thumbnail sketch of each book that I recommend. Of course, this hardly represents a complete list of all the wonderful books that are available, but I believe this will help to get you started in the right direction:

1. As a Man Thinketh by James Allen, published by Hallmark Cards & Fleming H. Revell Co. - This little book (only 64 pages) is an inspirational development of "For as he thinketh in his heart, so is he..." Proverbs: 23.7. From Allen's Foreword, the object of his book is "... to stimulate men and women to the discovery and perception of the truth that they themselves are makers of themselves by virtue of the thoughts which they choose and encourage; that "mind" is the master-weaver, both of the inner garment of character and the outer garment of circumstance, and that, as they may have hitherto woven in ignorance and pain, they may now weave in enlightenment and happiness." This book is a development of how thoughts and thought-forms affect our lives.

2. Thoughts are Things by Ed Walker, Yogi Pub. Co. - Another short book along the same lines, and well worth reading.

3. At the Feet of the Master by Alcyone, pub: Quest Books - This remarkable tiny book (a pocket size is available) was written by a thirteen year old who later changed his name to Krishnamurti. Krishnamurti is the Indian philosopher whom I spoke about earlier in this book. There is an interesting story that goes along with Alcyone and the writing of this book.

It seems that when Alcyone was quite young he came into association with Annie Besant and Charles Leadbeater, two of the world's most renowned clairvoyants who lived in the early part of the 20th century, and when they saw this little boy, Alcyone, they observed that his aura was so large and so pure that they were convinced that he would be the vehicle for the second coming of the Christ and so they took him under their wing to raise and educate him under the purest of circumstances. Alcyone, of course, was not involved with the Christ second coming, but nevertheless turned out to be one of the great men of our century.

While being cared for by Besant and Leadbeater this young man came under the tutelage of one of the Masters, and, as he says in his introduction, "These are not my words; they are the words of the Master who taught me." There is such wisdom and beauty in this little book that if one just followed all the instructions within it, one would lead a life of fulfillment and would make great gains along The Path that leads to the Kingdom.

4. The Prophet by Kahlil Gibran, pub. by Alfred Knopf - One of the most beautiful books ever written. It is filled with Metaphysical wisdom. If you haven't read this, you are in for a rare treat.

5. Siddhartha by Hermann Hesse, Pub. Bantam Books - Another short book, in the form of a novel. The story parallels the life of Gautama Buddha even though the Buddha appears briefly as a character in the story. It is the story of an individual who spends many years following false paths until finally realizing their fruitlessness and eventually finds Nirvana (another name for the Kingdom).

6. The Secret Life of Plants by Tompkins and Bird, published by Avon Books - This book contains the story of Cleve Backster as well as many other interesting facts about plants.

7. Thought Forms by Besant and Leadbeater, published by Quest Books - Annie Besant and Charles Leadbeater, as I mentioned above, were two of the most renowned clairvoyants of the twentieth century who joined forces to write this book about thought forms. Much of the material that I used in describing thought forms comes from this book (and the next one). These two books are a must read.

8. Man Visible and Invisible by Leadbeater, published by Quest Books - This book, along with *Thought Forms*, give you a good idea of the workings of the Emotional and Mental bodies.

9. Astral Plane by Leadbeater, published by Quest Books - An in depth study of the Astral Plane.

10. Thought Power by Annie Besant, published by Quest Books - A much more in depth study of the power of thought and how it affects your life.

11. Metaphysics: The Science of Life by Anthony J. Fisichella, published by LLewellyn - This is one of the most thoughtful and insightful books ever written on the subject. I say this as a matter of fact and not just because "Tony" was my mentor and friend. Although the book is out of print, copies are still available by emailing Doug@Higher-Ground.com or website: http://www.higher-ground.com. Tony just recently passed on to the next plane but his work continues through his son Doug.

12. Reincarnation, an East-West Anthology by Cranton and Head, published by Quest Books - The title speaks for itself.

13. Illusions: The Journeys of a Reluctant Messiah by Richard Bach, published by Avon Books - This is a fun novel about a Messiah who needs to get away from all the people asking him for things and pulling on his clothes. He ends up as a companion to a barnstorming pilot and as they travel around the country he reveals many Metaphysical teachings.

CONCLUSION

In the spirit of "always leave them laughing." I leave you with this: It seems that there was this gentleman, let's call him John, who decided that the direction of his life was leading him to join a monastic order. The monastery that he chose had strict rules concerning vows of silence and the members of this order were allowed to say only two words every five years. The head monk was completely satisfied that John understood this and thus he was allowed to join the Order.

Soon enough, the five years were up and John reported to the head monk to say his two words, and they were, "Bed's hard."

Another five years passed and this time his words were, "Food's bad."

Yet another five years go by and John's words were, "I quit!" Whereupon the head Monk replied, "It's about time. All you've done since you got here is complain!"

It is my sincerest hope that you will have gained a great comfort and joy in knowing that there is a Grand Purpose to your life and that you are part of a Grand Evolutionary Scheme, and that you have within you the Power to further that Evolution.

In addition, no matter what your walk of life, know that you matter very much, for as part of God, God would not be complete without you. God Bless You.

www.ingramcontent.com/pod-product-compliance
Lightning Source LLC
Chambersburg PA
CBHW051804040426
42446CB00007B/515